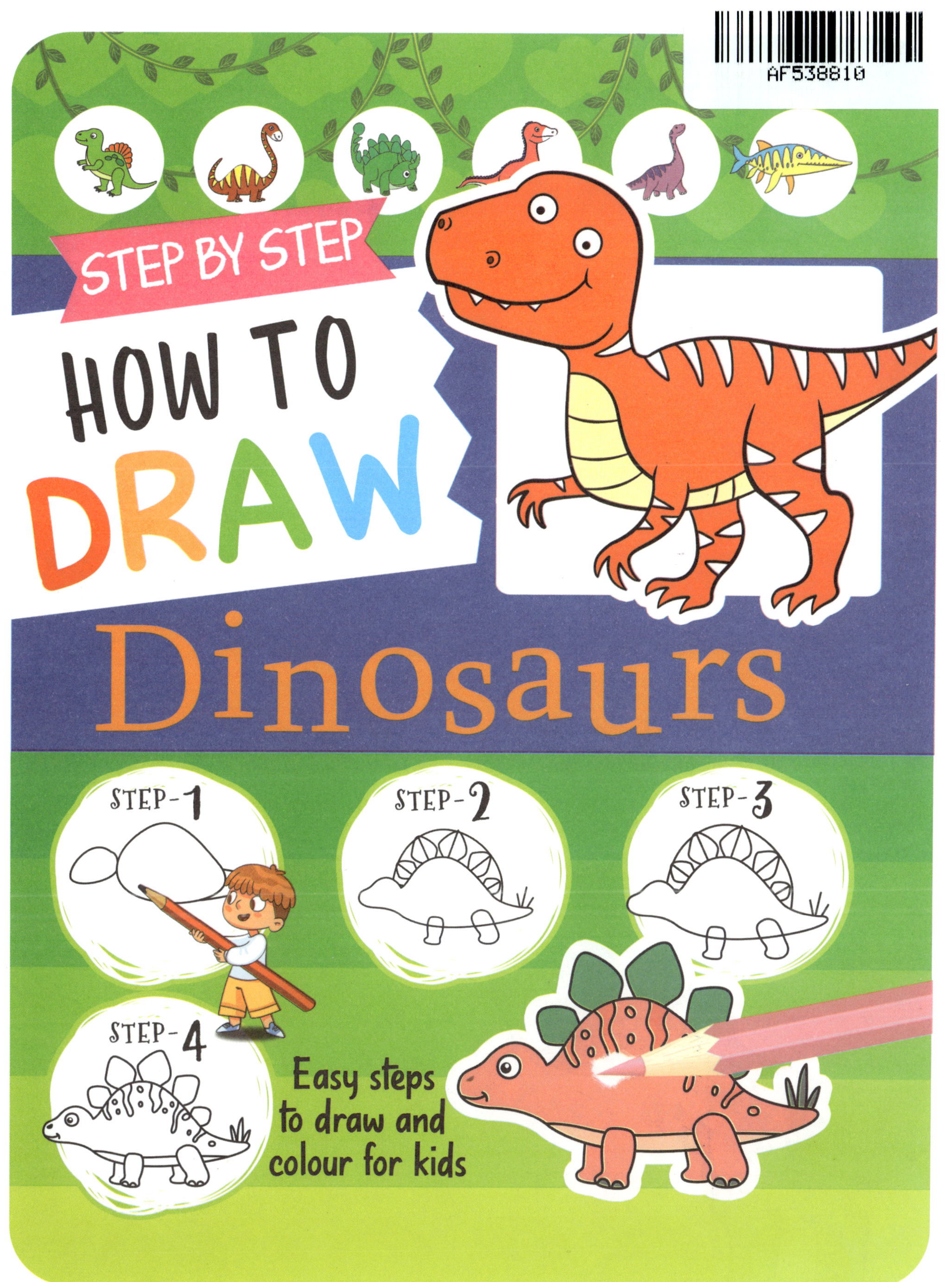
AF538810
STEP BY STEP
HOW TO DRAW
Dinosaurs
STEP-1
STEP-2
STEP-3
STEP-4
Easy steps to draw and colour for kids

TYRANNOSAURUS

This is a Tyrannosaurus Rex. Its name means tyrant lizard king.

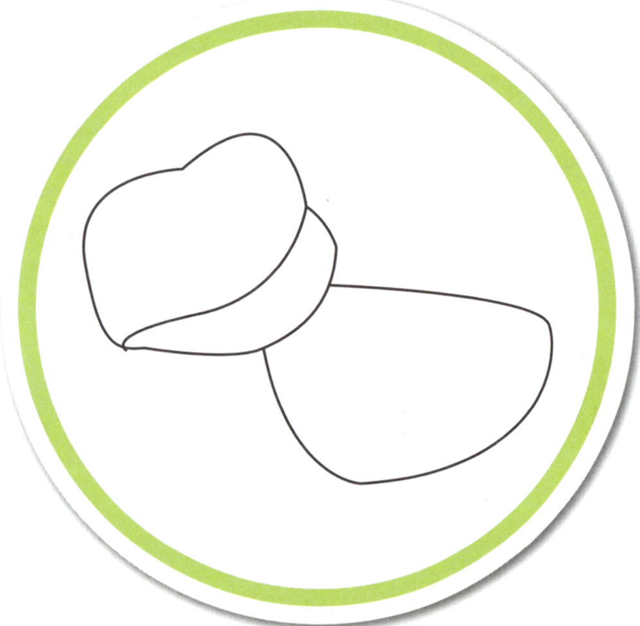

1 Draw the shape of a cap for the head and another shape of a wing at the back for the body.

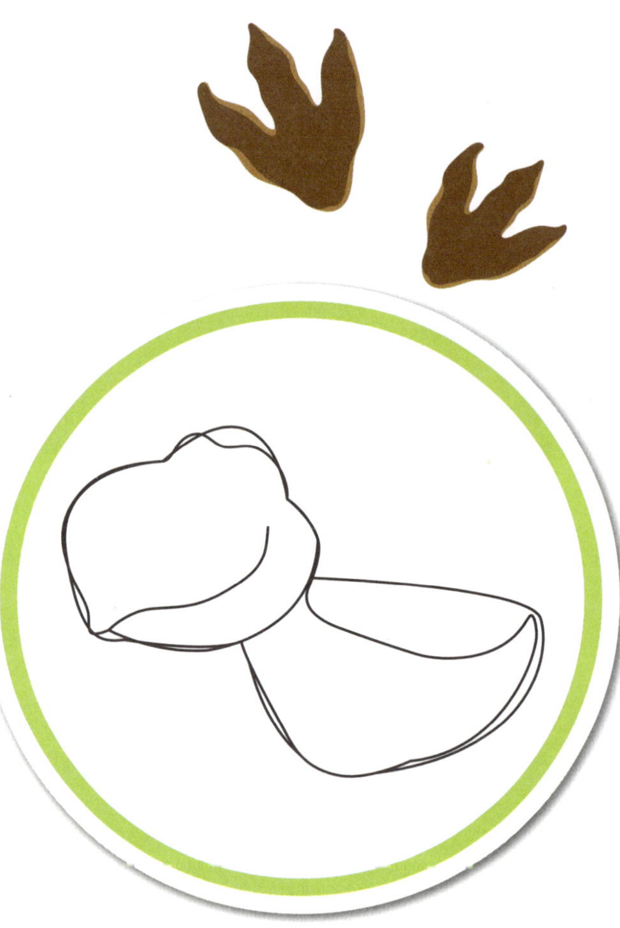

2 Curve the outlines a bit for the eyes and mouth. Curve the back part of the body.

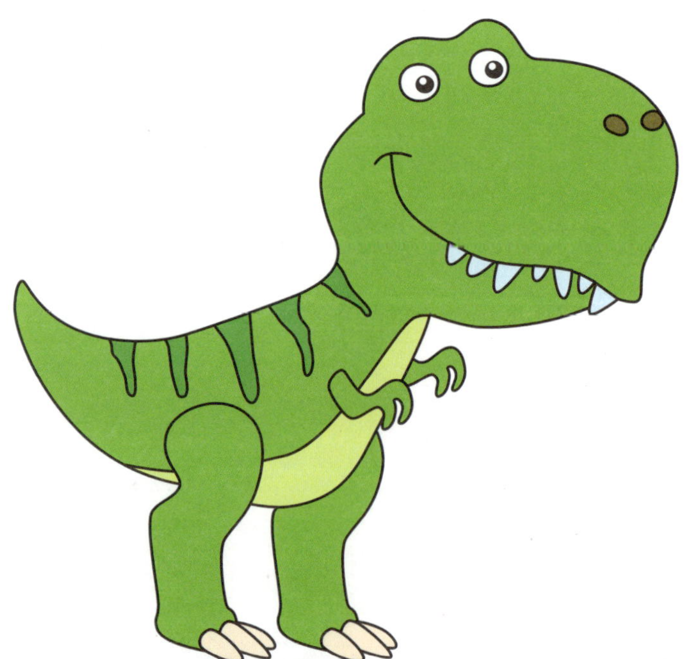

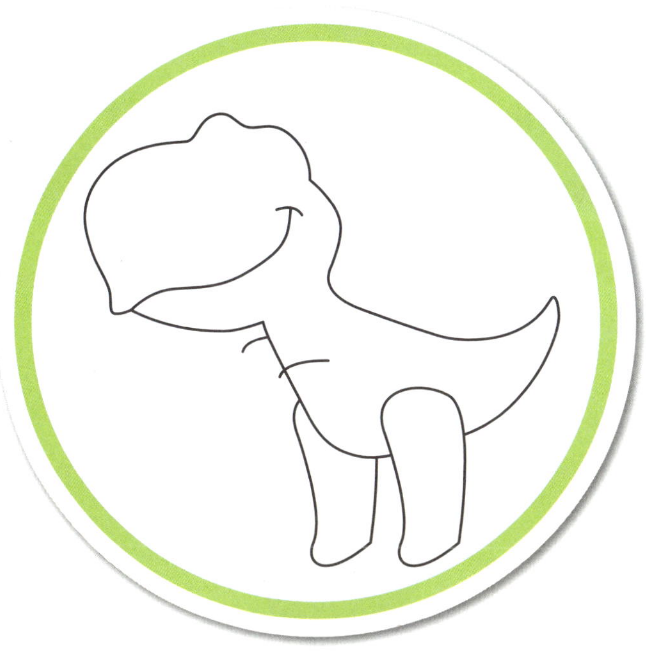

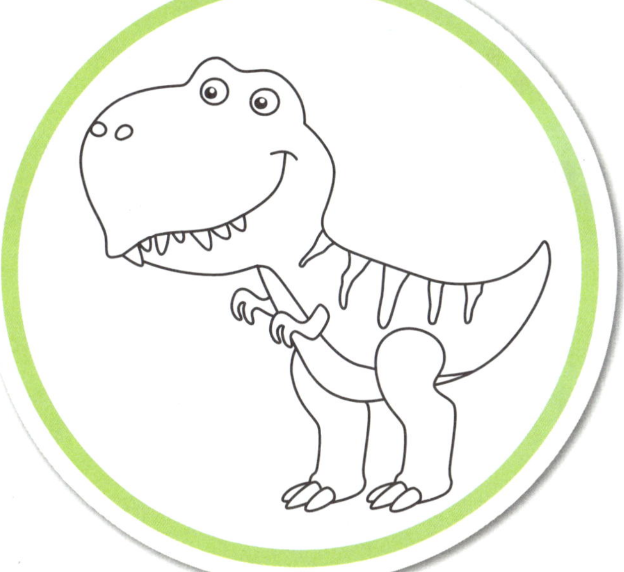

4 Draw circles for eyes and nostrils. Fill in the eyes. Draw teeth, stripes, arms, legs and feet.

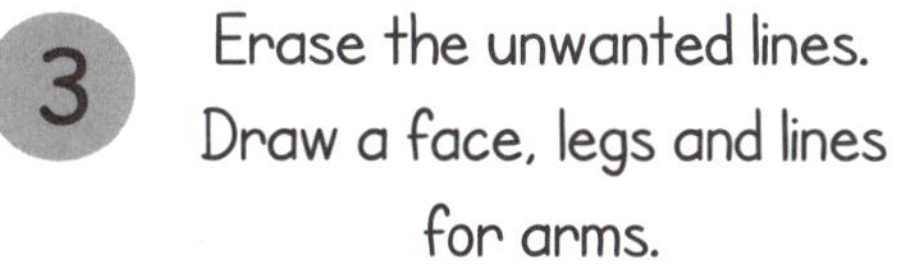

3 Erase the unwanted lines. Draw a face, legs and lines for arms.

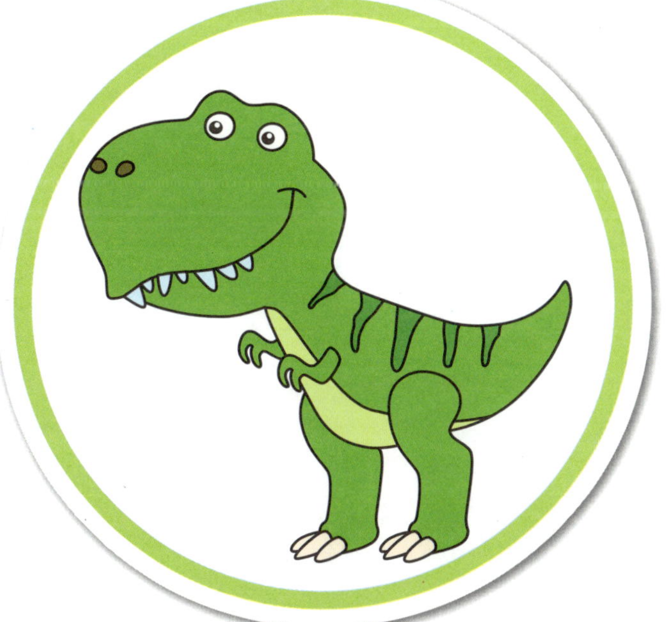

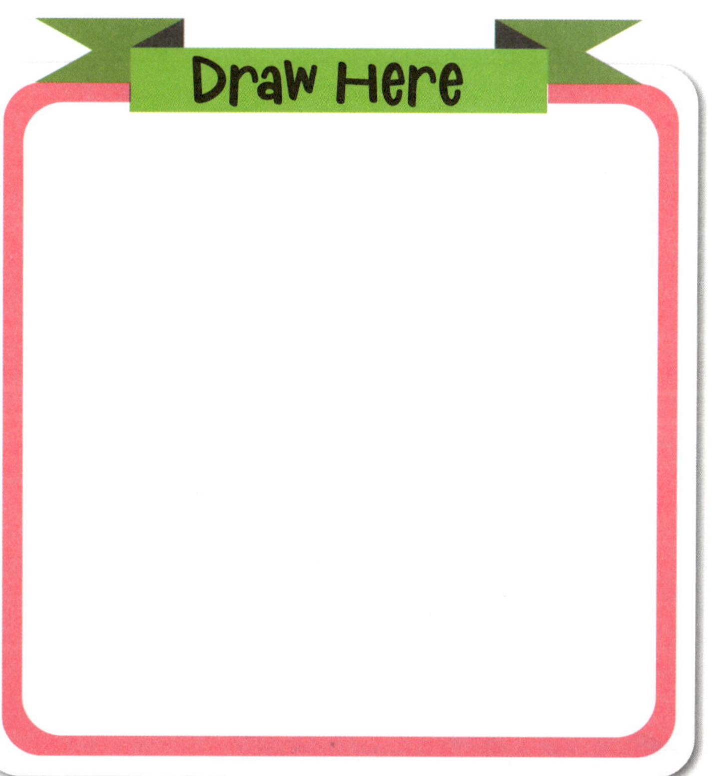

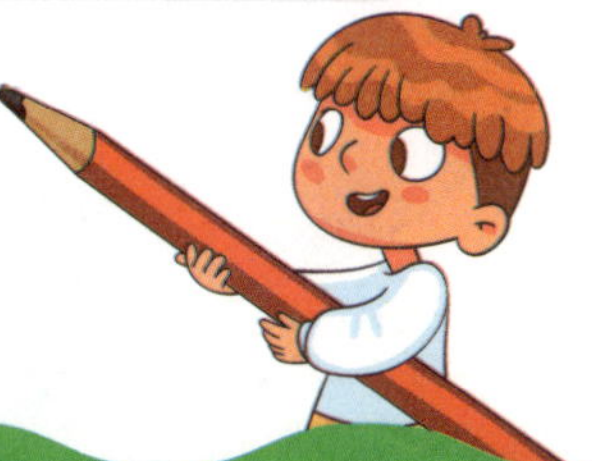

DIPLODOCUS

This is a Diplodocus. It was a herbivore and one of the longest dinosaurs.

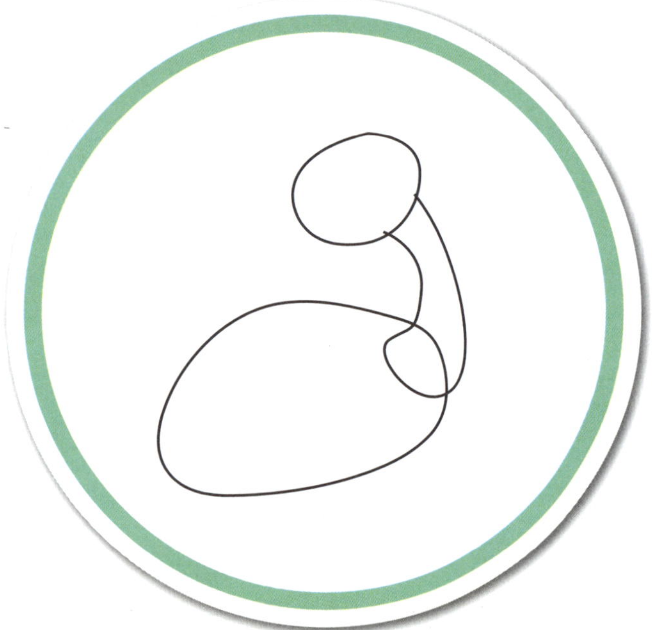

1 Draw an egg shape for the face and join it with another bigger egg shape for the body.

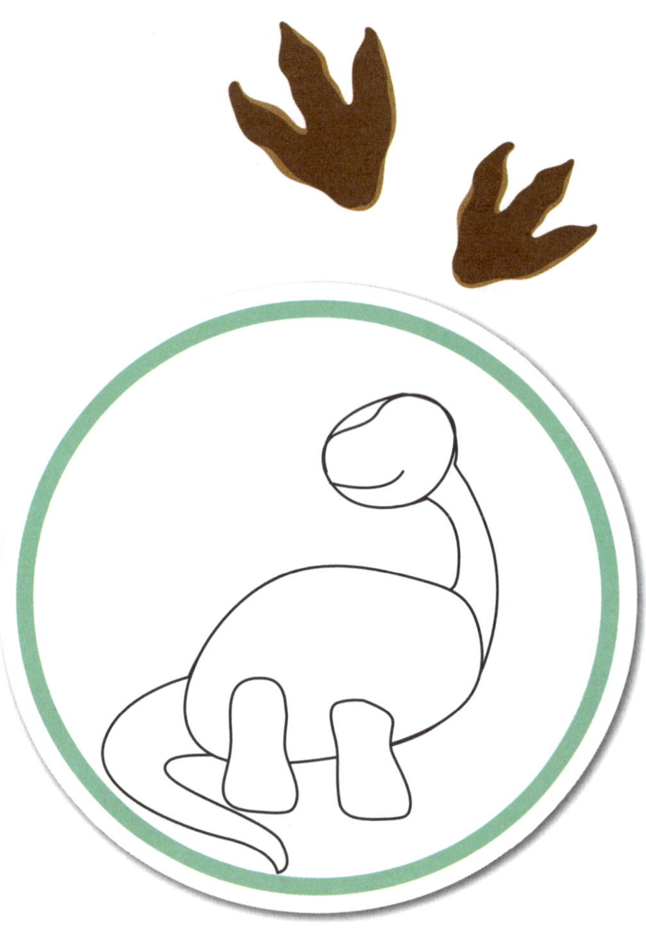

2 Draw a tail and its legs.

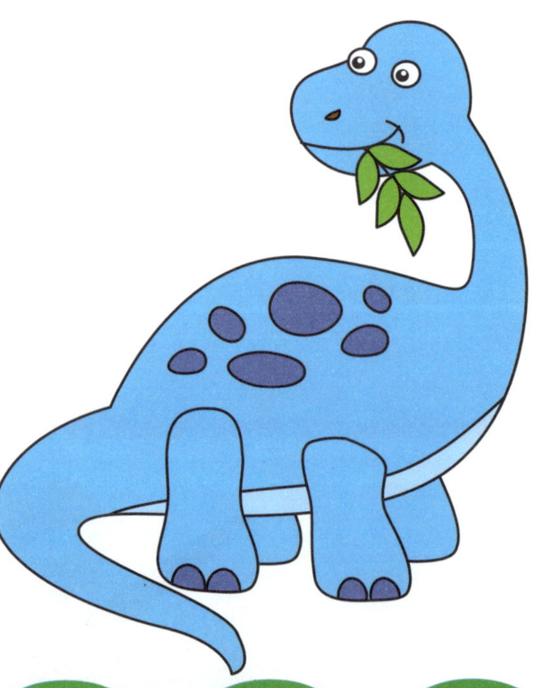

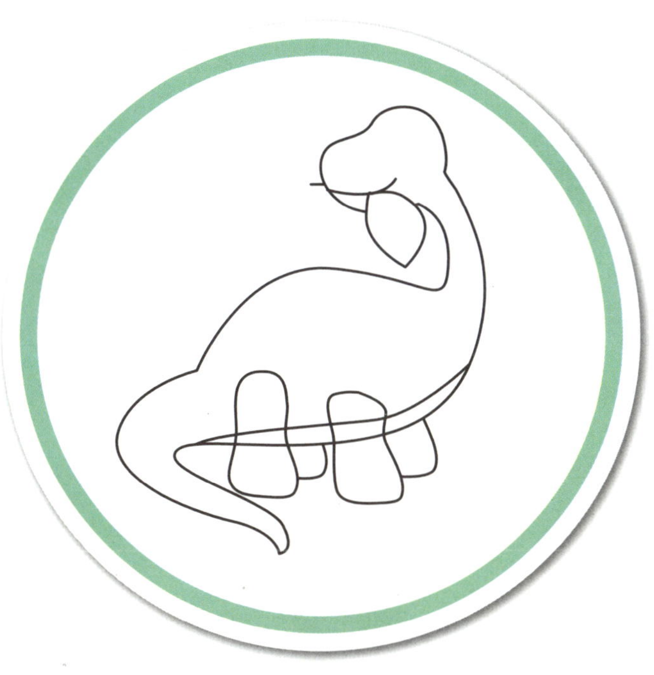

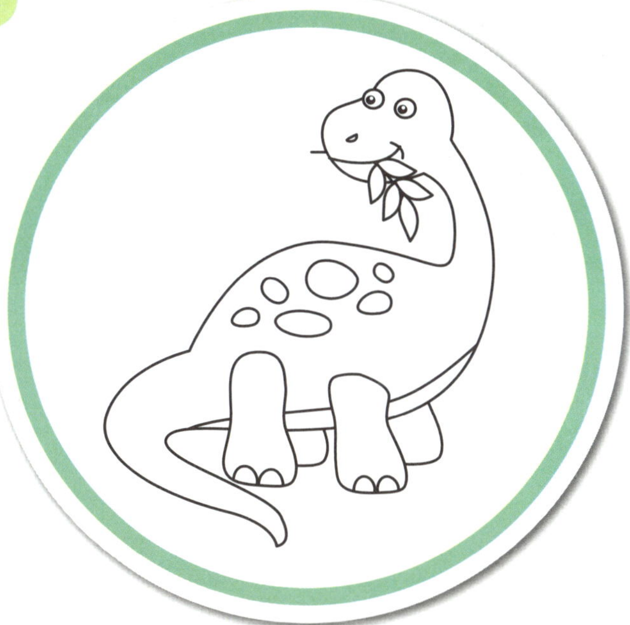

4 Divide the big leaf into small leaves. Fill in the eyes, draw toes and colour to complete.

3 Draw a leaf shape in its mouth. Erase unwanted lines. Curve the head and draw eyes, nose, mouth and spots on the body.

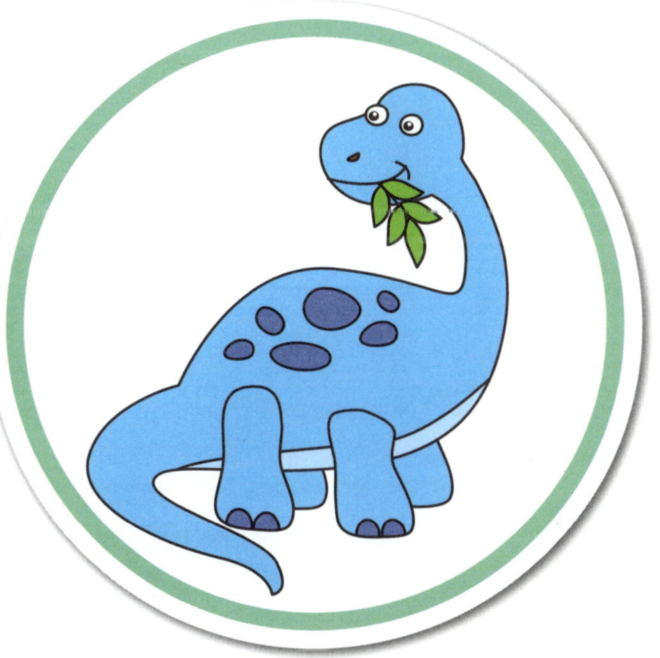

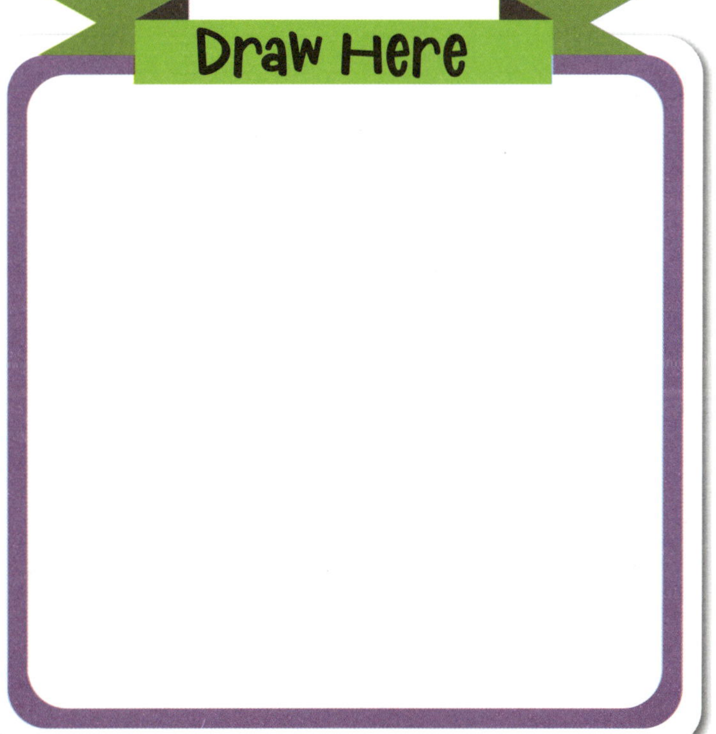

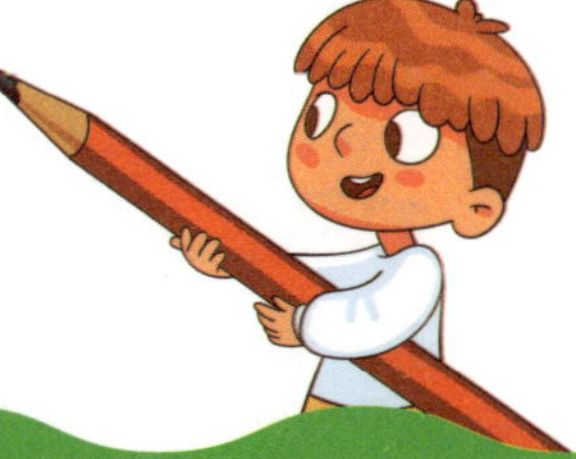

PARASAUROLOPHUS

This is Parasaurolophus. It had a long, bony crest on its head.

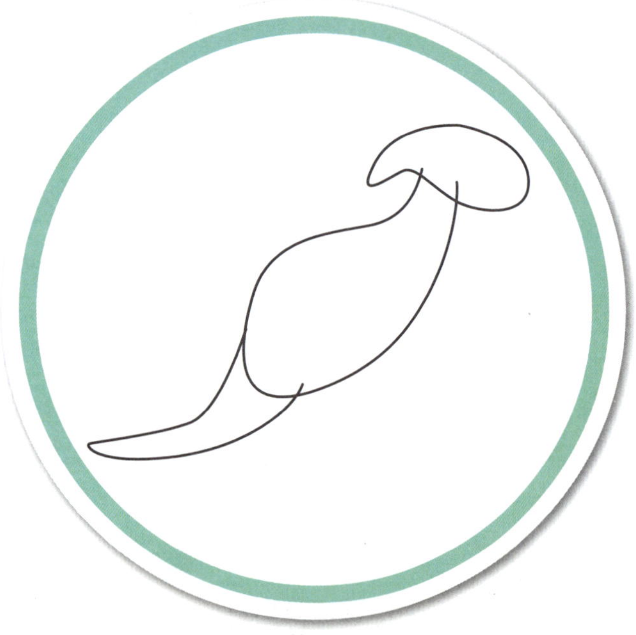

1 Draw an oval shape with a curve at the end for the crest. Draw a body and a tail.

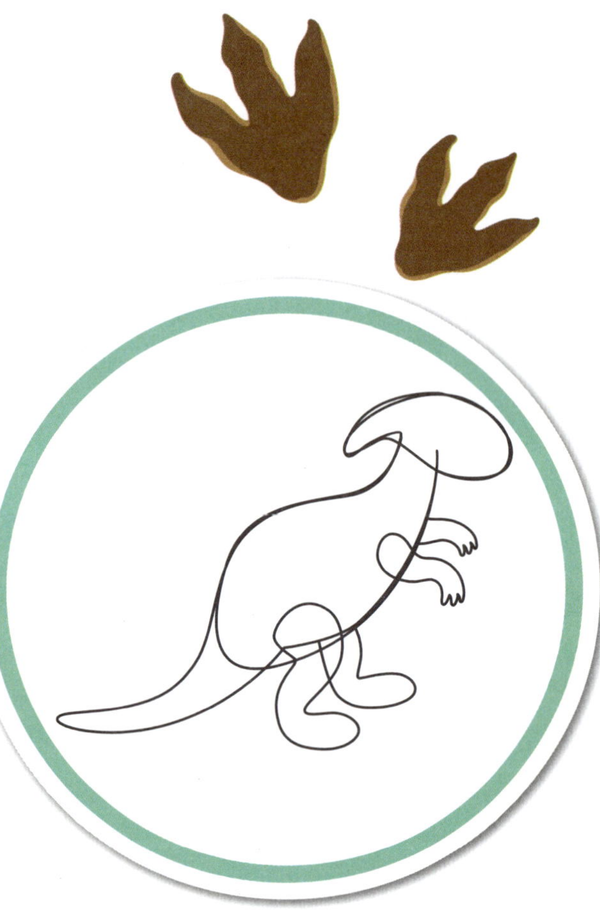

2 Darken the outline of the head and body. Draw arms and legs.

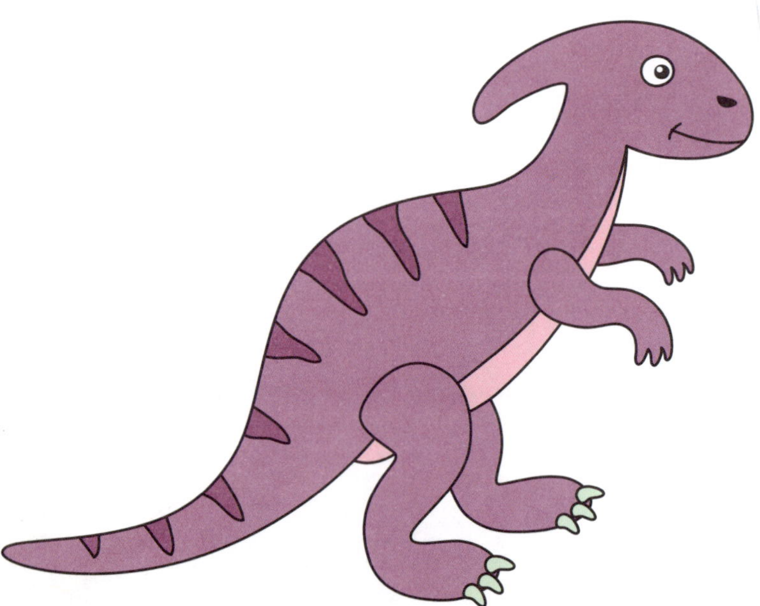

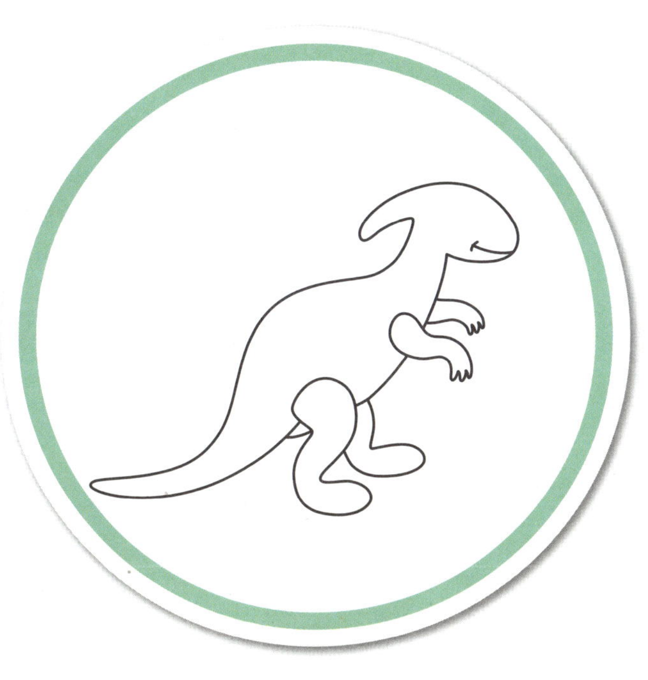

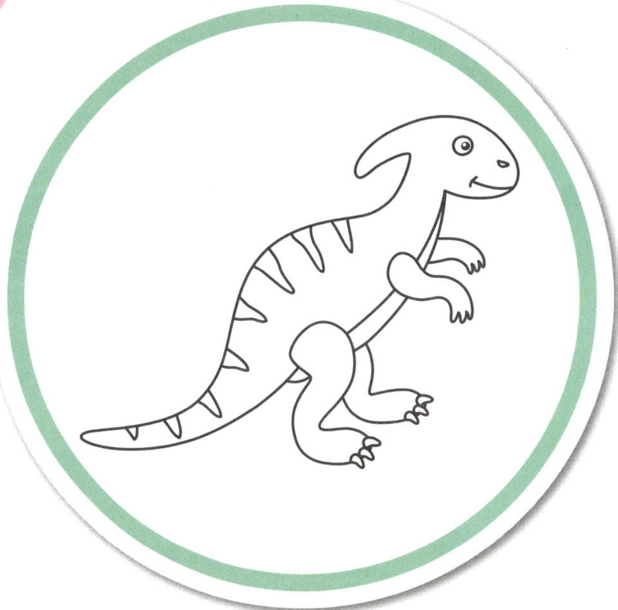

4 Draw an eyeball and fill in the eye. Draw stripes and a curved line for the body.

3 Draw a mouth and erase unwanted lines.

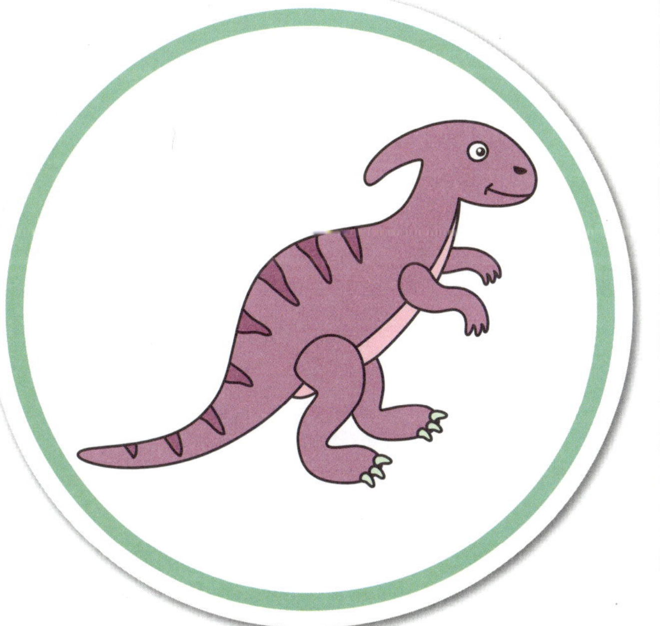

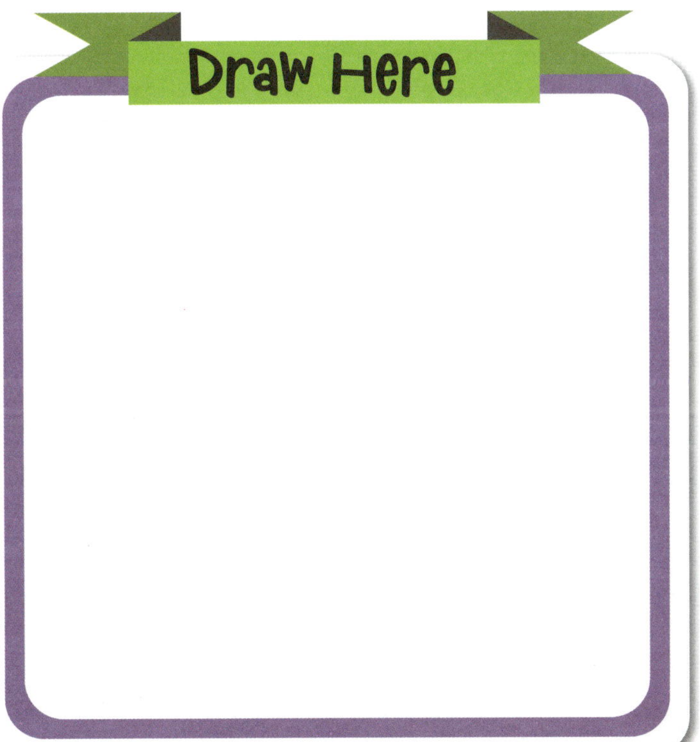

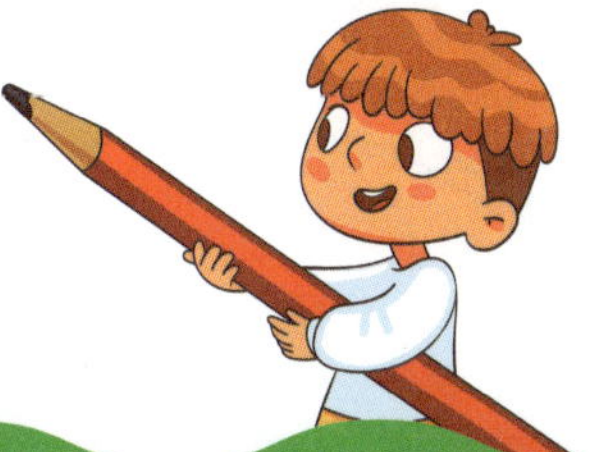

PTERODACTYL

This is a Pterodactyl. Some of them had wingspans of more than 36 feet.

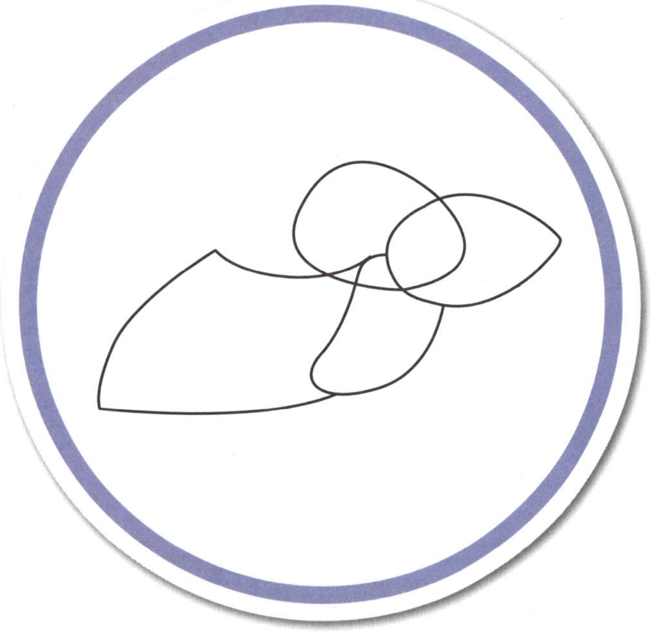

1 Draw an egg shape. On it, draw a leaf shape. From the egg shape, make a shape for the wing and body.

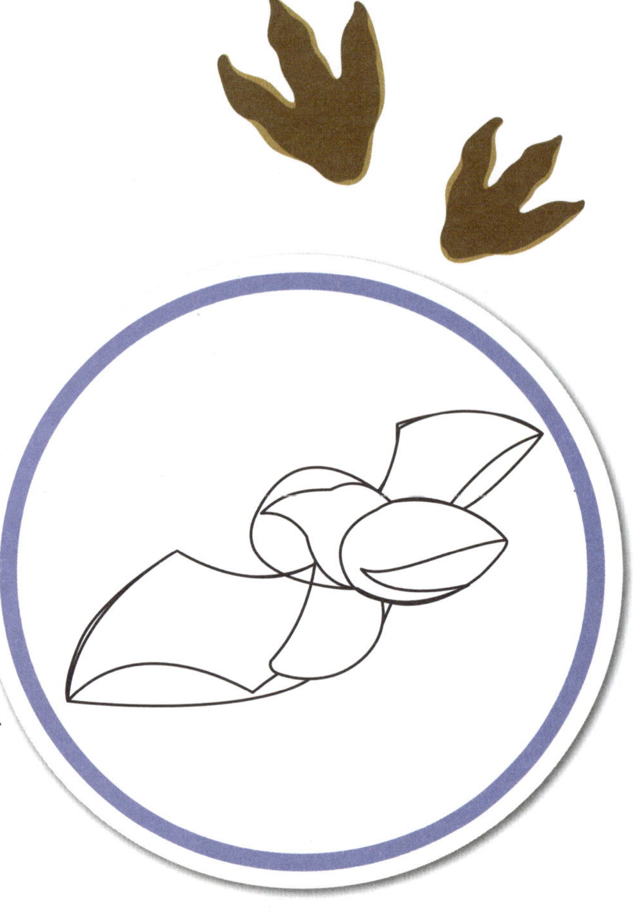

2 Draw another wing. Draw lines to make the face, beak and curves to give shape to the left wing.

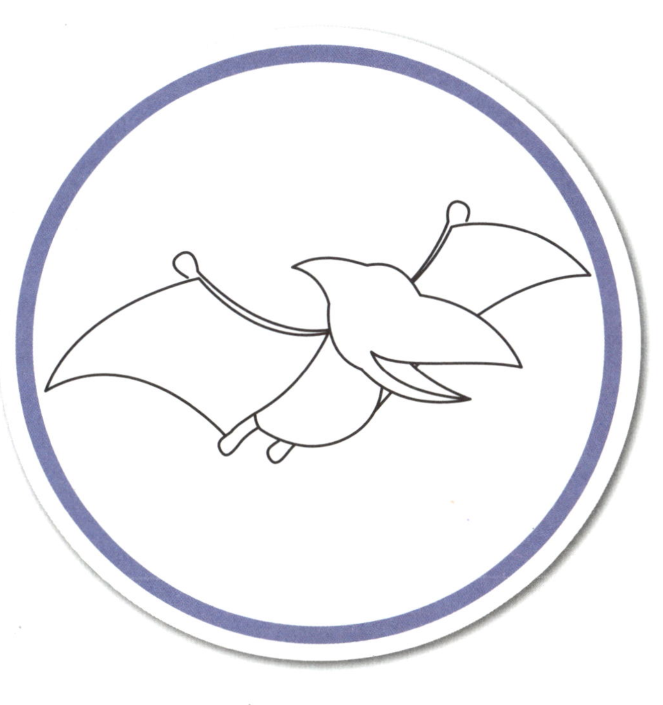

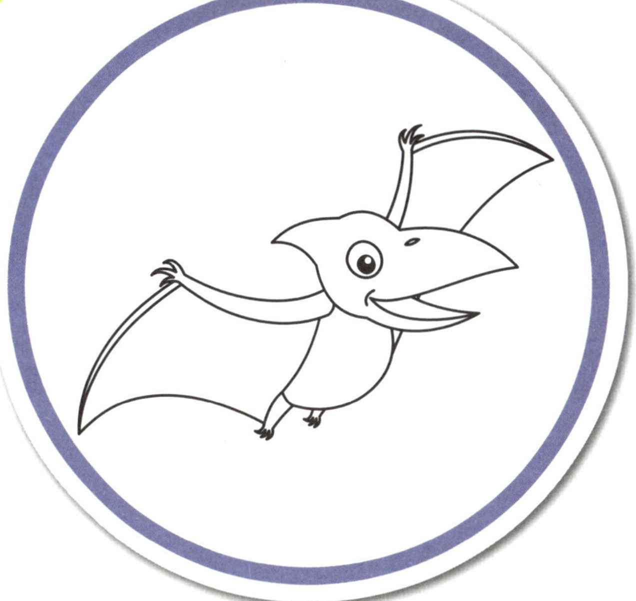

4 Draw an eye and fill it. Draw the nose, claws of the hands and legs. Colour to complete.

3 Draw lines to make hands alongside the wings. Draw legs.

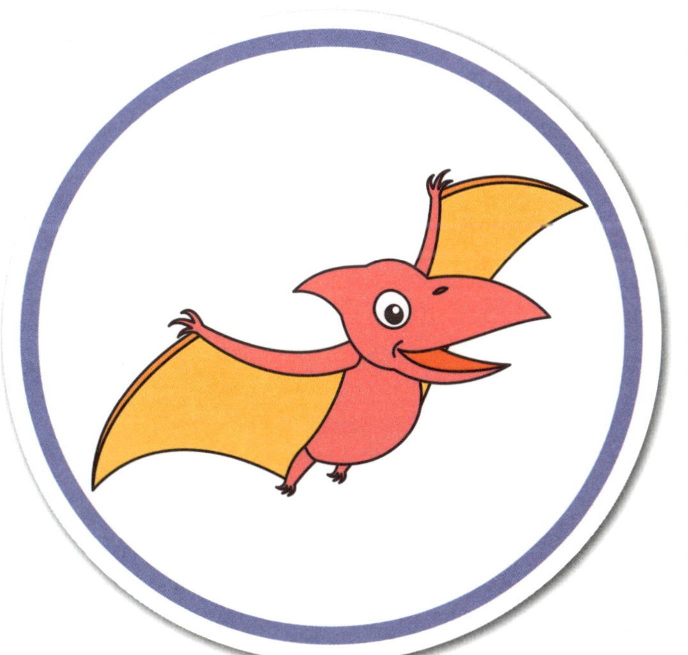

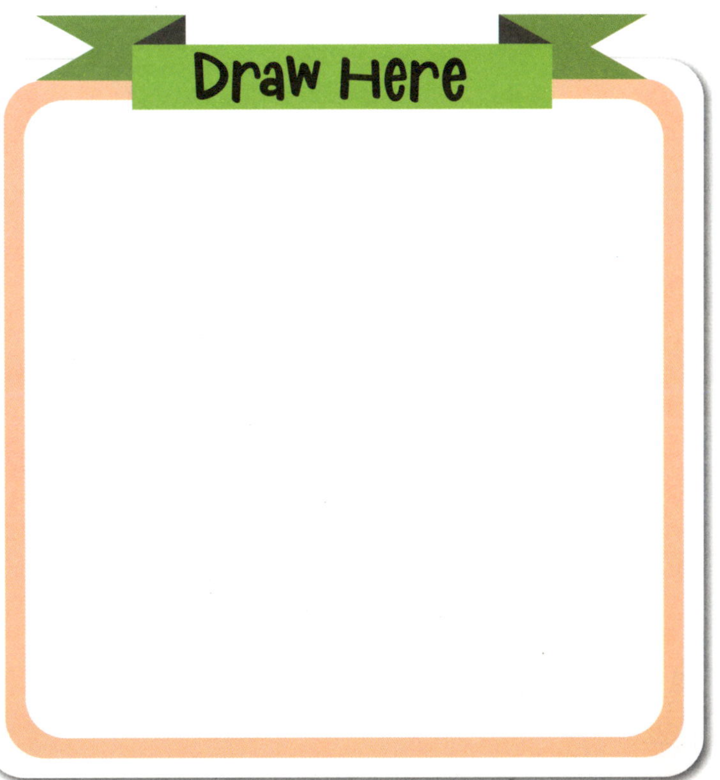

STEGOSAURUS

This is Stegosaurus. It had bony plates on its back.

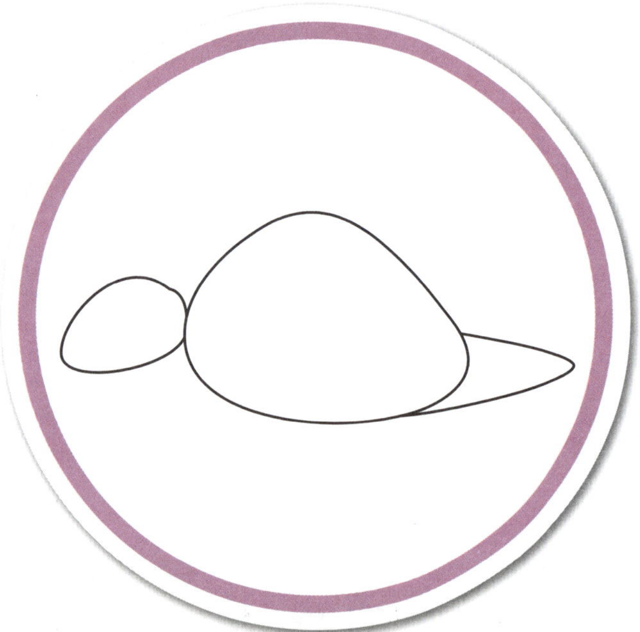

1 Draw an egg shape for the head and a bigger egg shape for the body. A curved triangle for the tail.

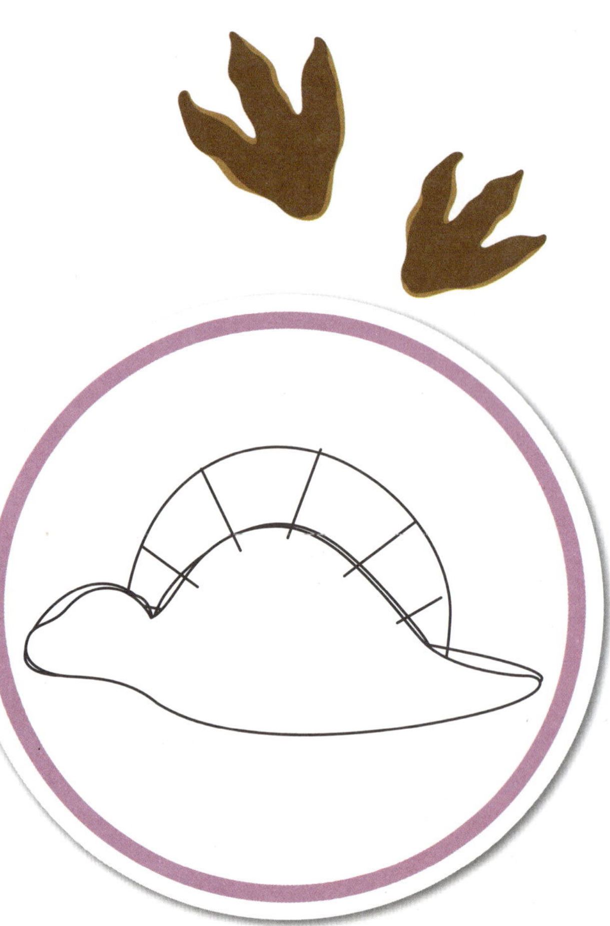

2 Curve the outlines to give it shape. Draw a semi-circle with lines in between, like the shell of a snail.

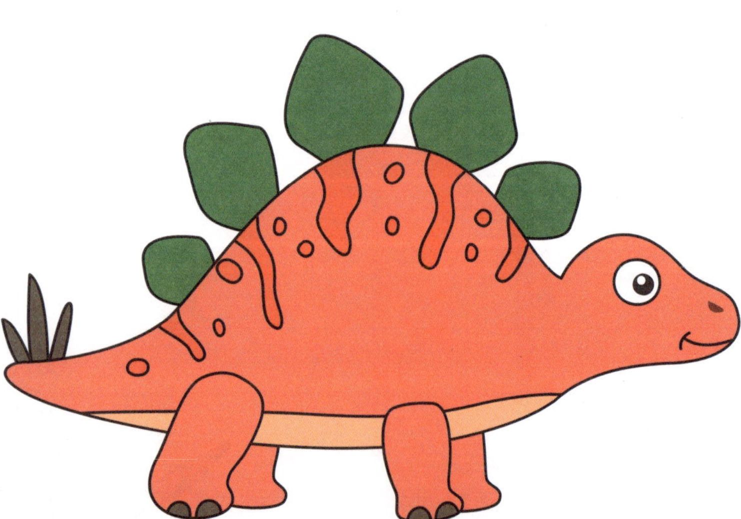

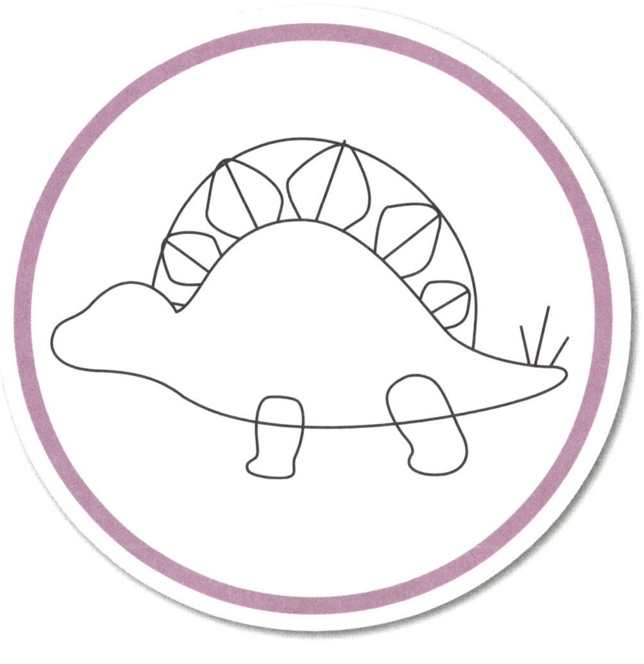

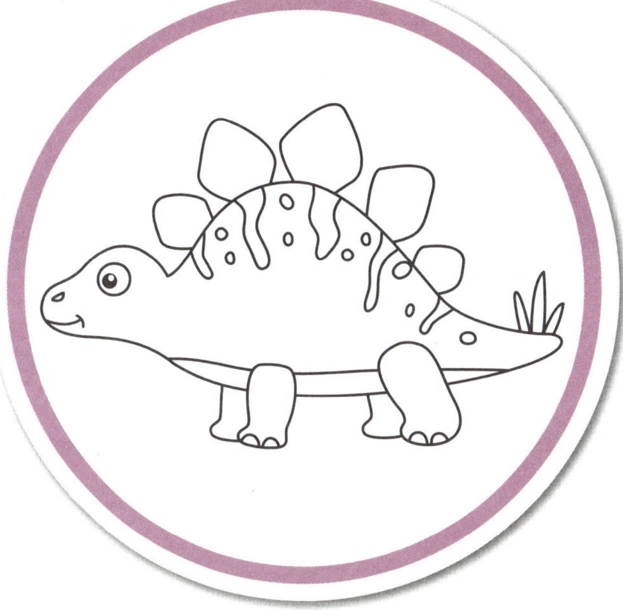

4 Draw an eye, nostril, mouth and circles for spots and wavy lines for stripes. Draw legs. Colour to complete.

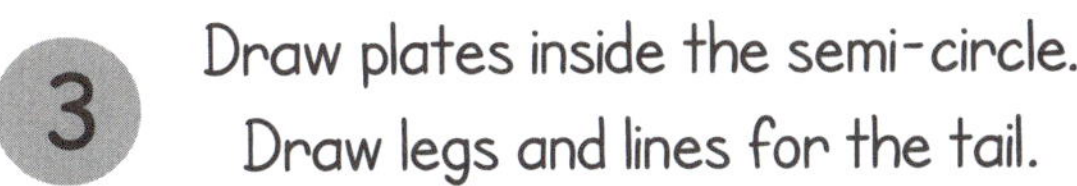

3 Draw plates inside the semi-circle. Draw legs and lines for the tail.

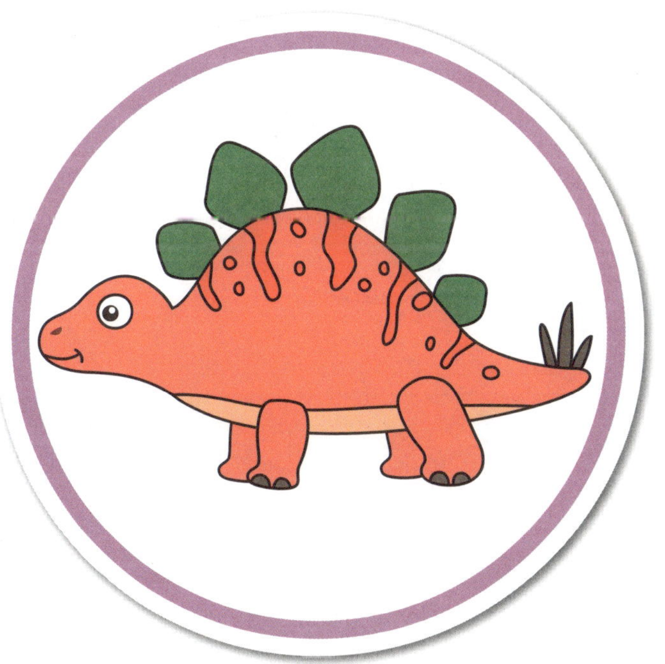

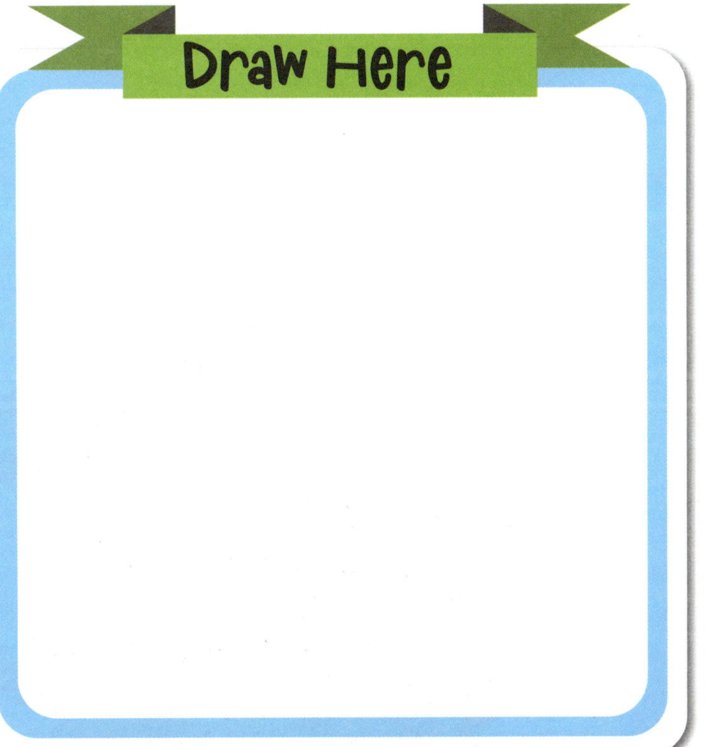

SPiNOSAURUS

This is Spinosaurus. It had a massive sail on its back.

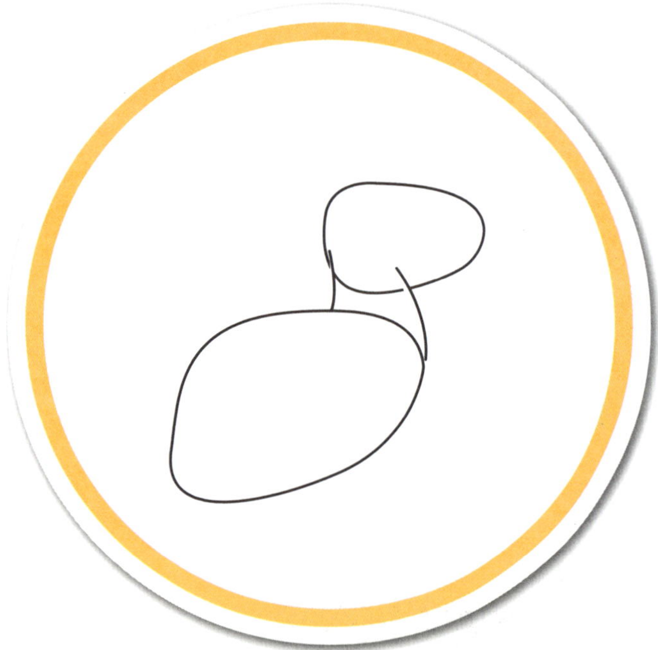

1 Draw an egg shape that is flat at the bottom for the face. Draw the neck and body.

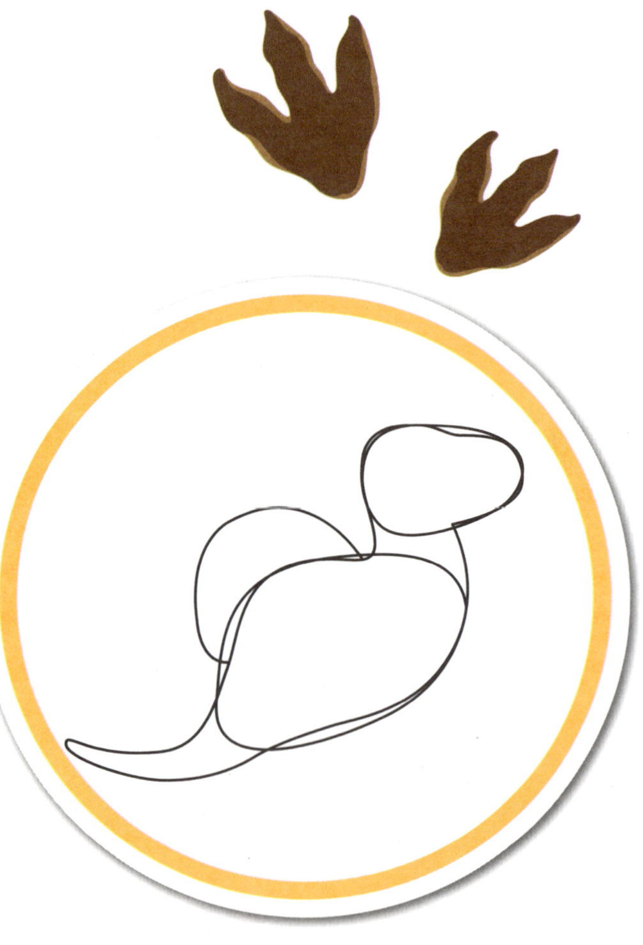

2 Curve the outlines to give a definite shape. Draw a tail and a semi-circle for the sail on the back.

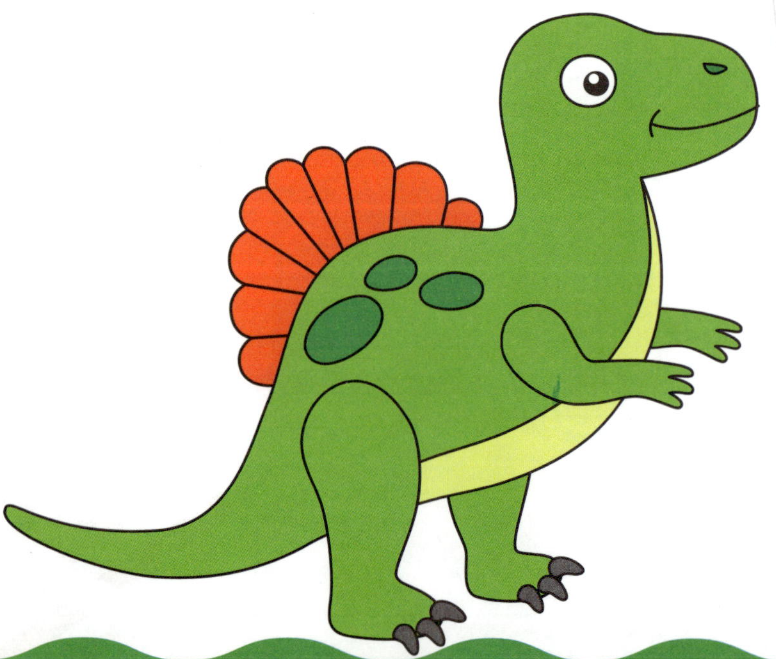

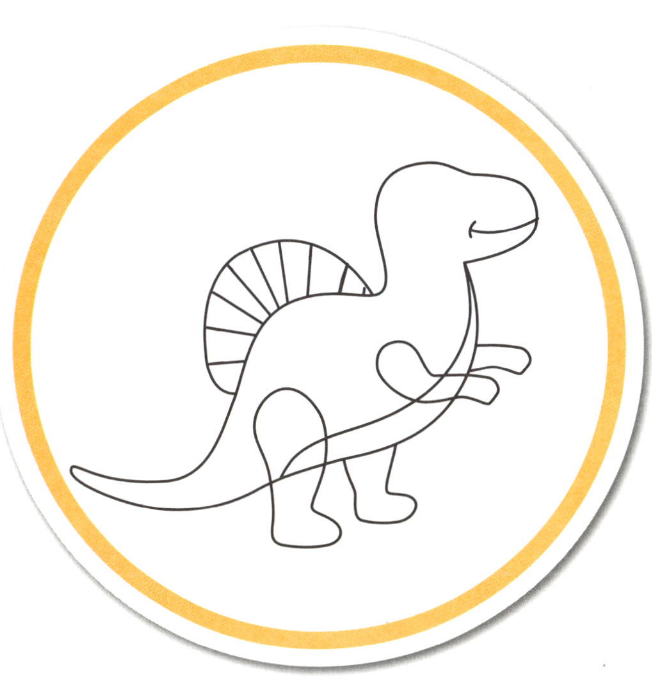

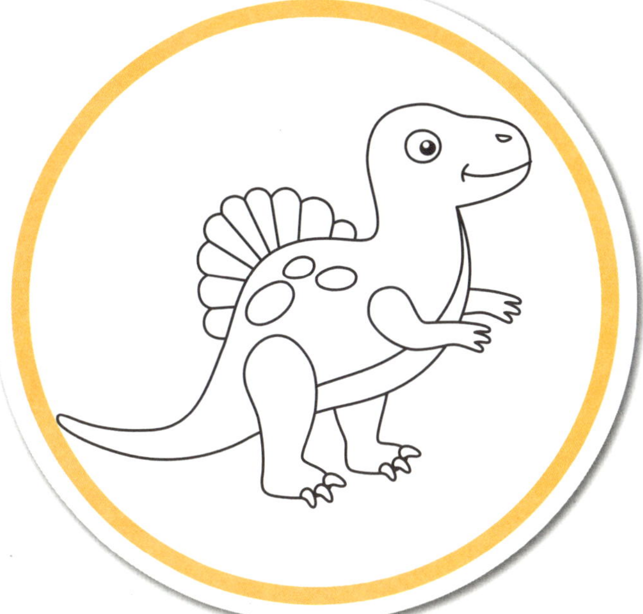

4 Draw a nostril. Curve the sail. Draw circles on the body. Draw the toes and nails. Erase unwanted lines.

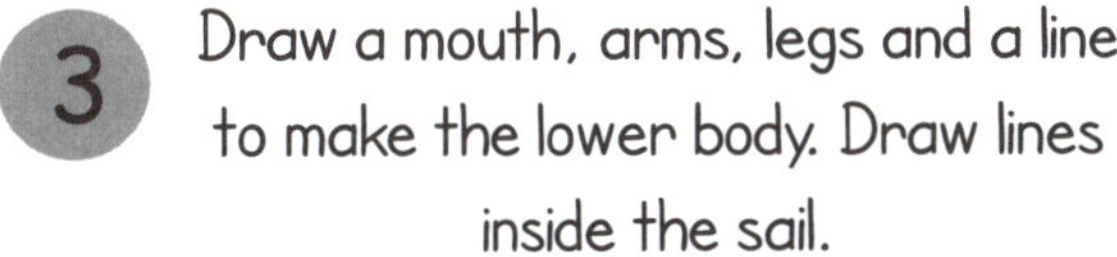

3 Draw a mouth, arms, legs and a line to make the lower body. Draw lines inside the sail.

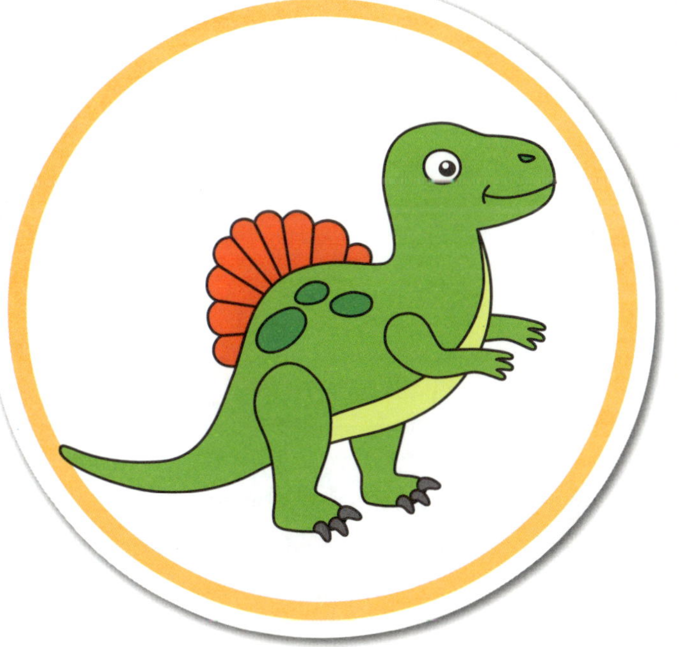

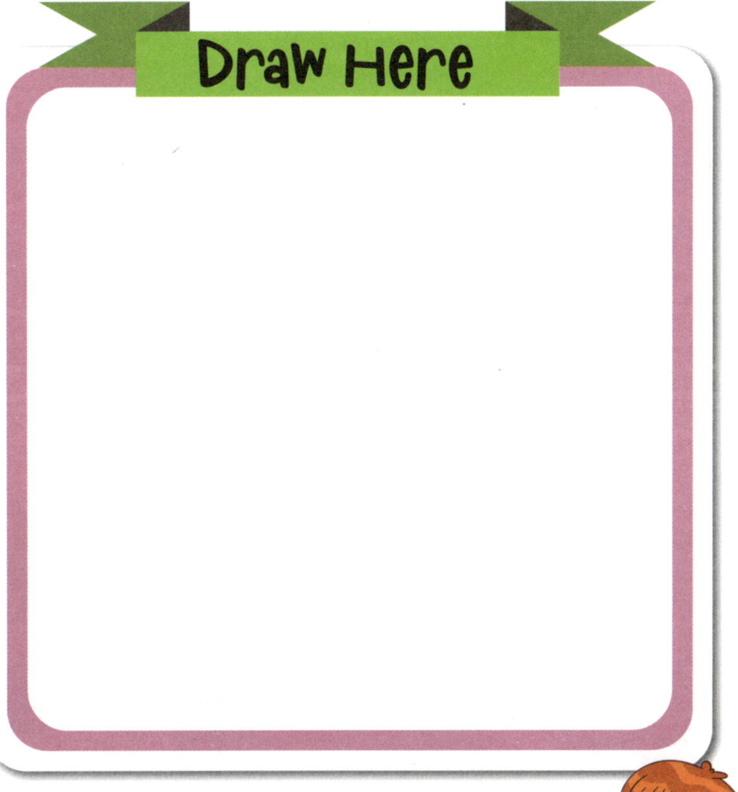

TRICERATOPS

This is Triceratops. It had a frill around its neck and three horns.

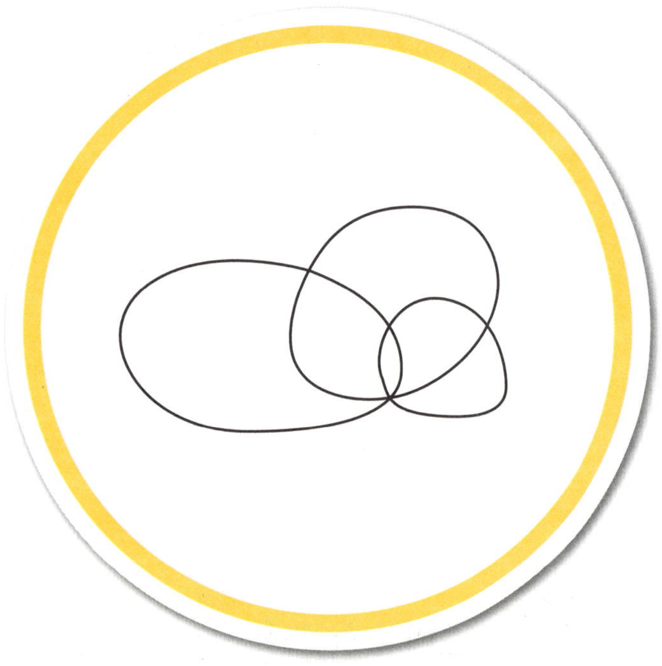

1 Draw an egg shape. At one end, draw an intersecting egg shape and a small stone shape.

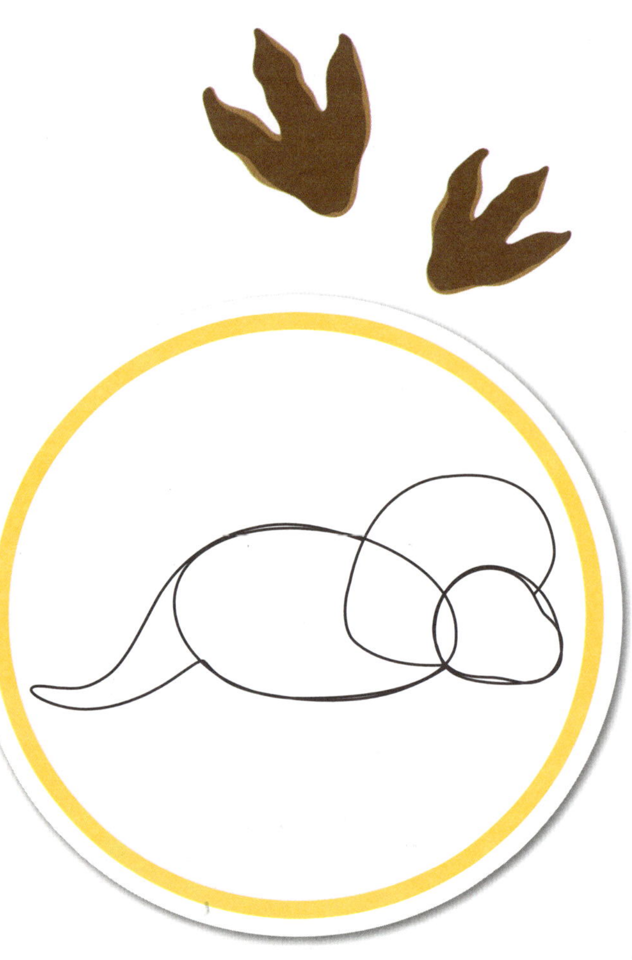

2 Draw a tail at the end of the egg shape. Outline to give a definite shape to the face and body.

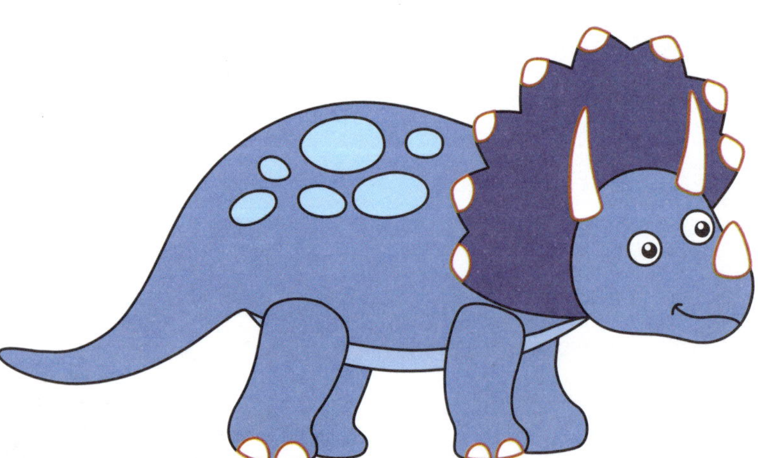

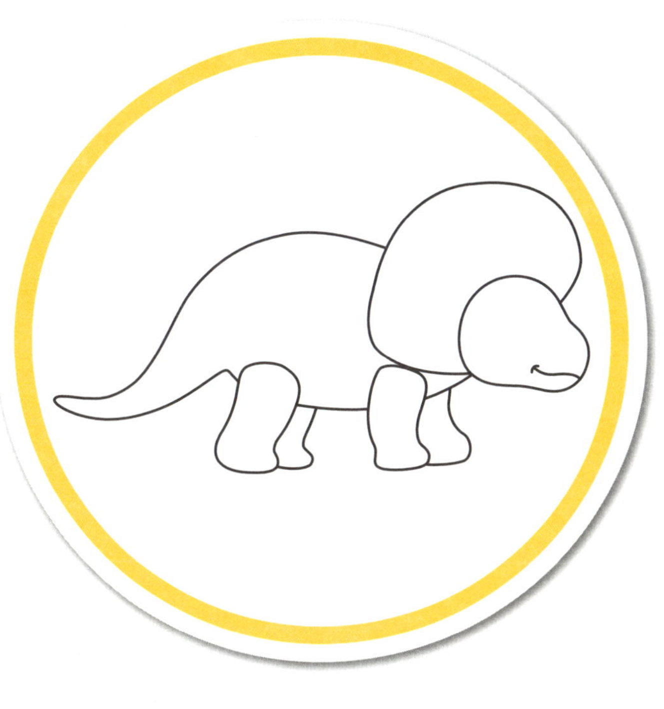

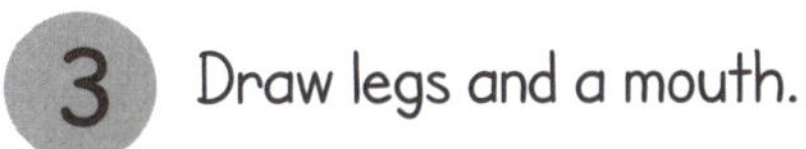

3 Draw legs and a mouth.

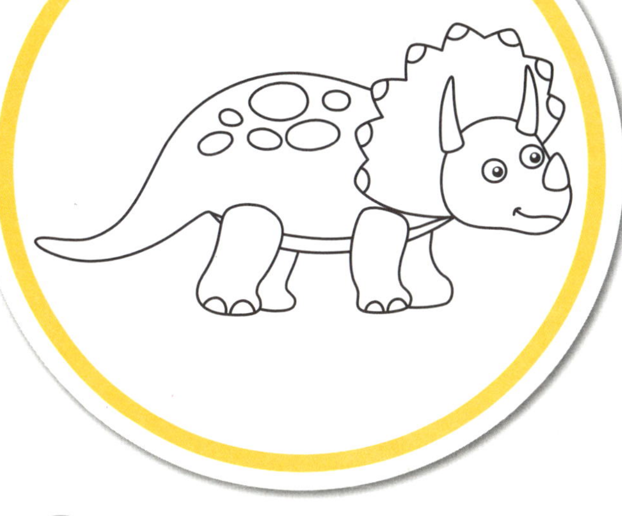

4 Draw eyes, horns, frill design, spots, toes and the lower body line. Colour to complete.

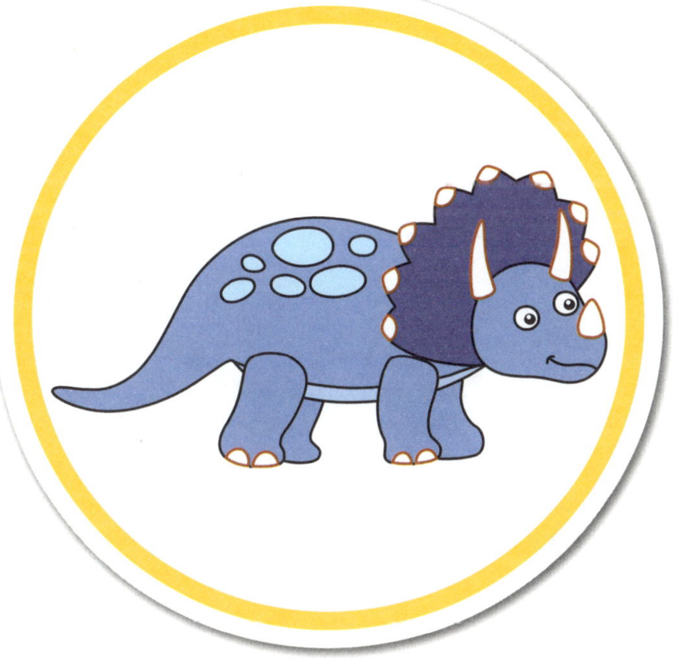

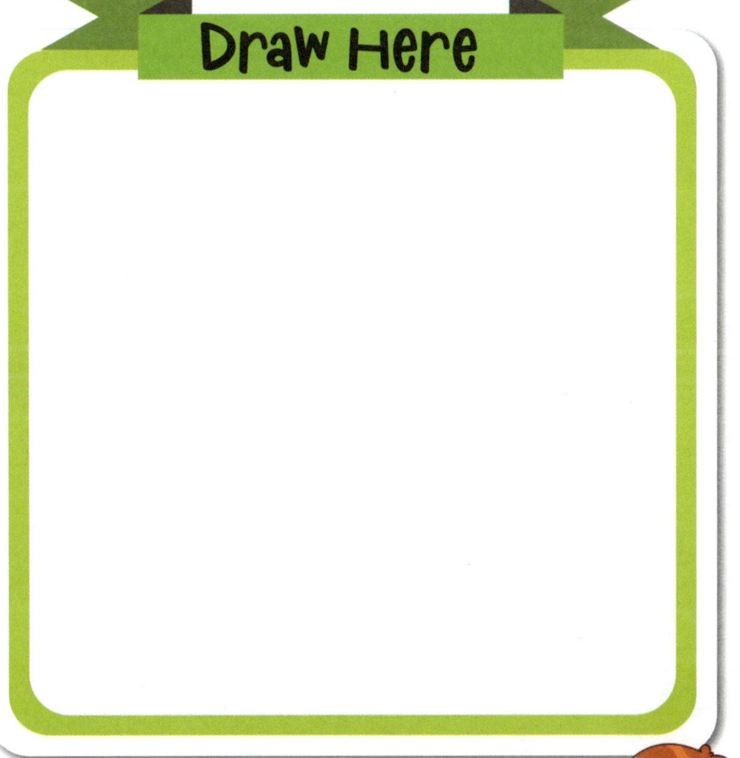

ELASMOSAURUS

This is Elasmosaurus. Its neck was five times the length of its trunk.

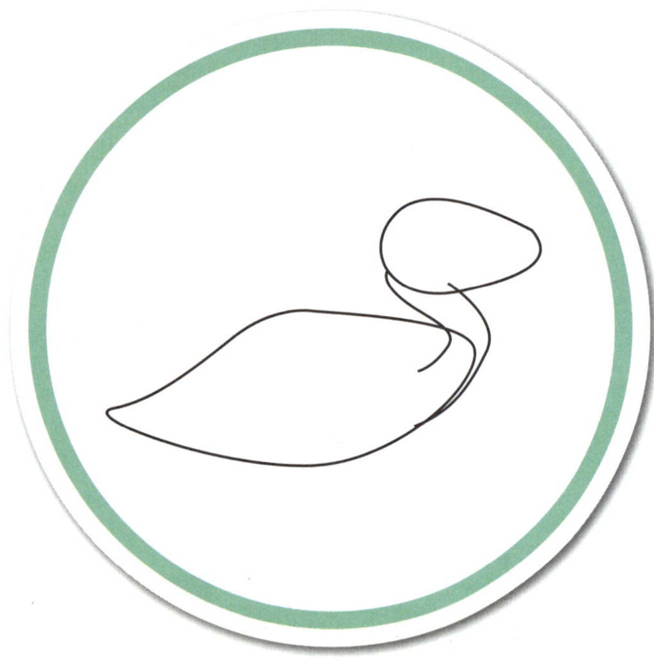

1 Draw an egg shape. Draw a curved neck and the shape of a duck's body.

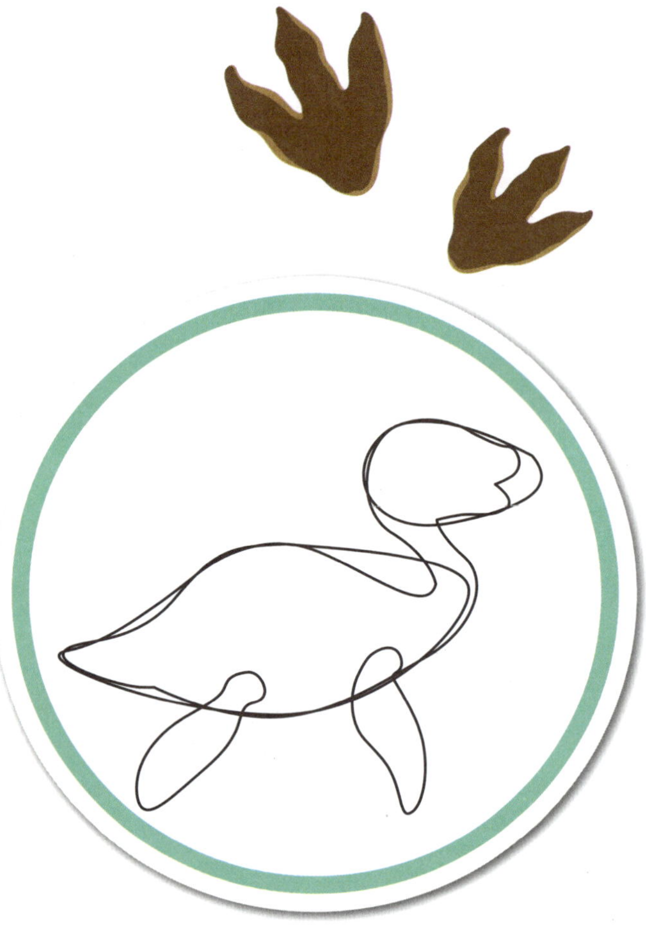

2 Outline to give a definite shape. Curve to make the mouth. Draw flippers.

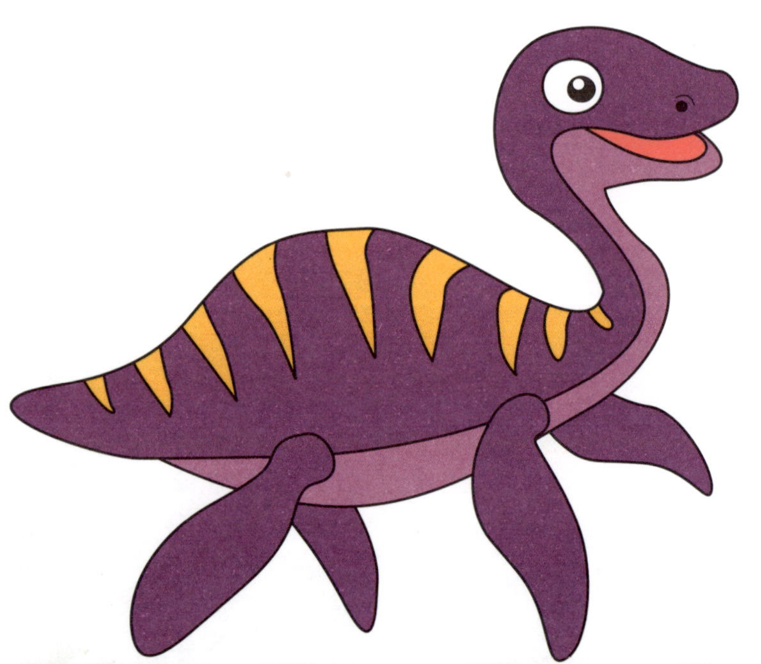

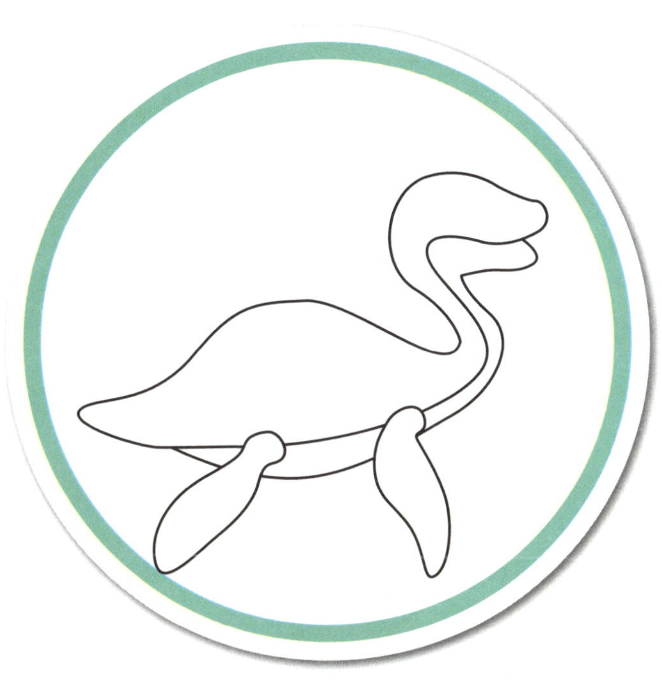

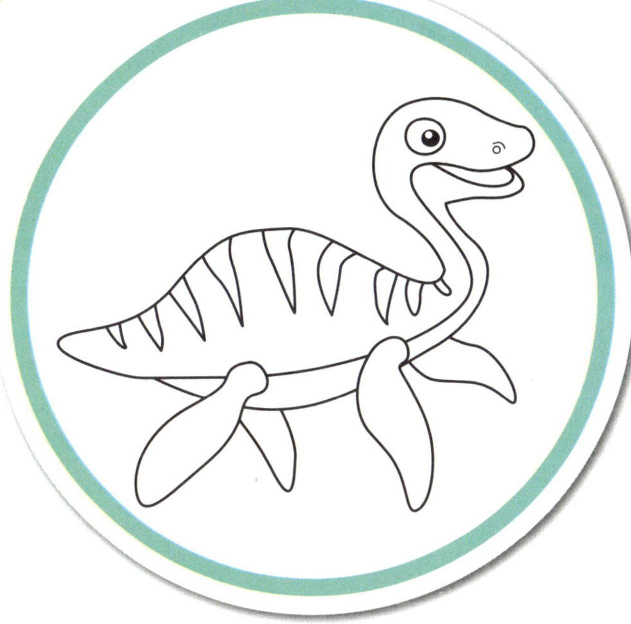

4 Draw the eye, nostril, stripes on the body and remaining limbs. Colour to complete.

3 Draw a double line from the mouth to the lower body.

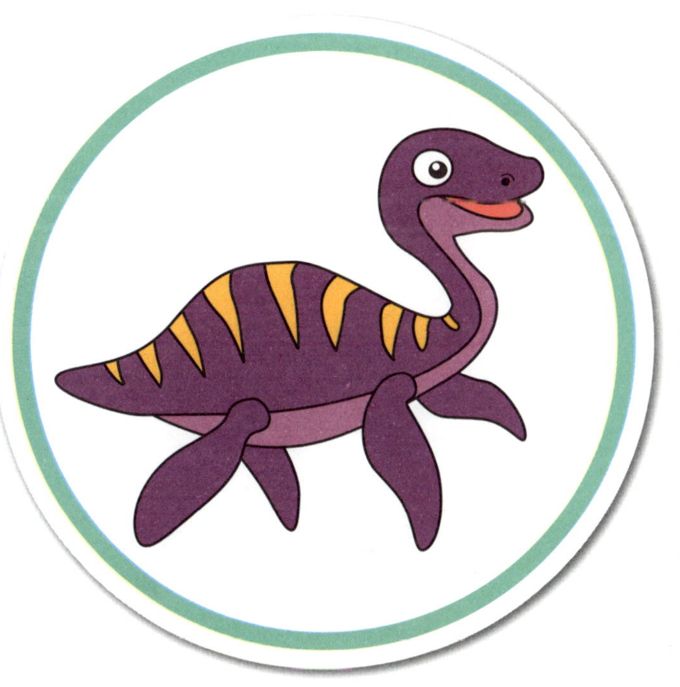

Draw Here

ALLOSAURUS

This is Allosaurus. It lived in the late Jurassic Period.

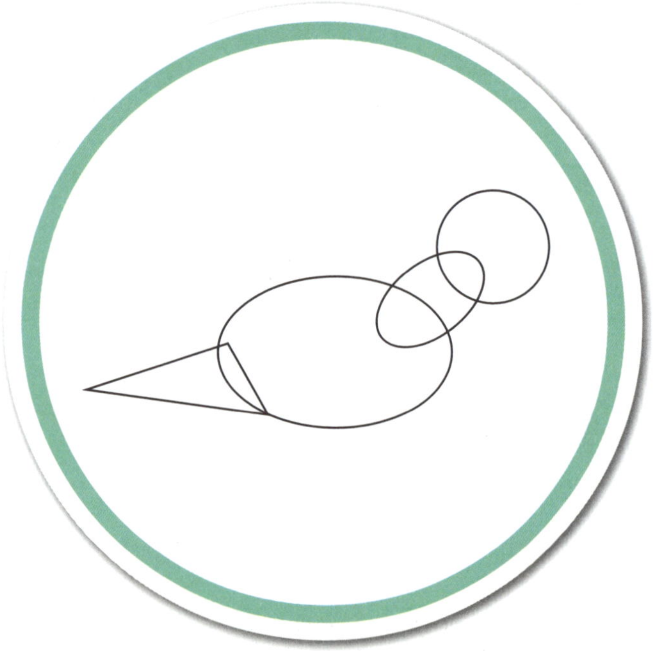

1 Draw a big oval and on its left, make a traingle. To its right, draw an egg shape and a circle above it.

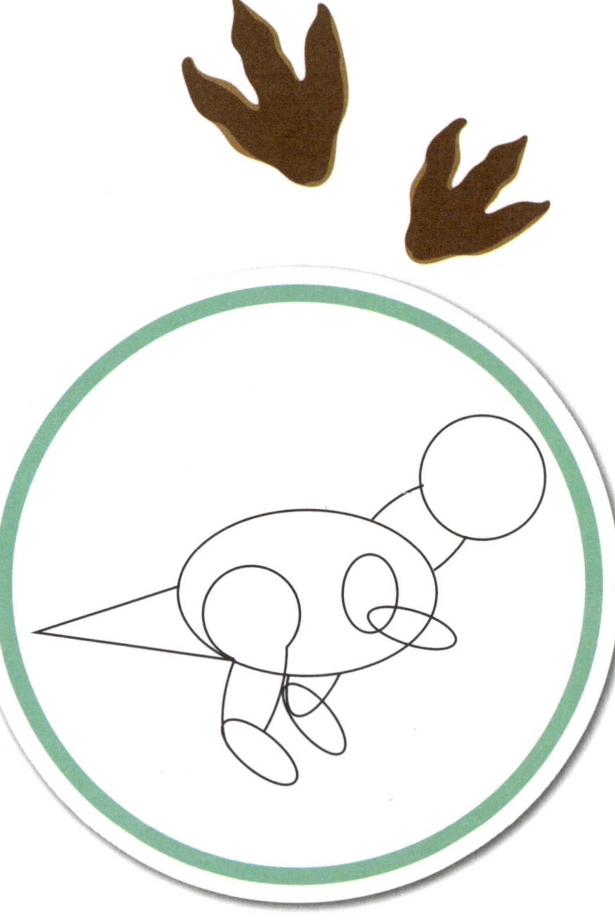

2 On the lower side of the big oval, draw legs and arms. Erase unwanted lines.

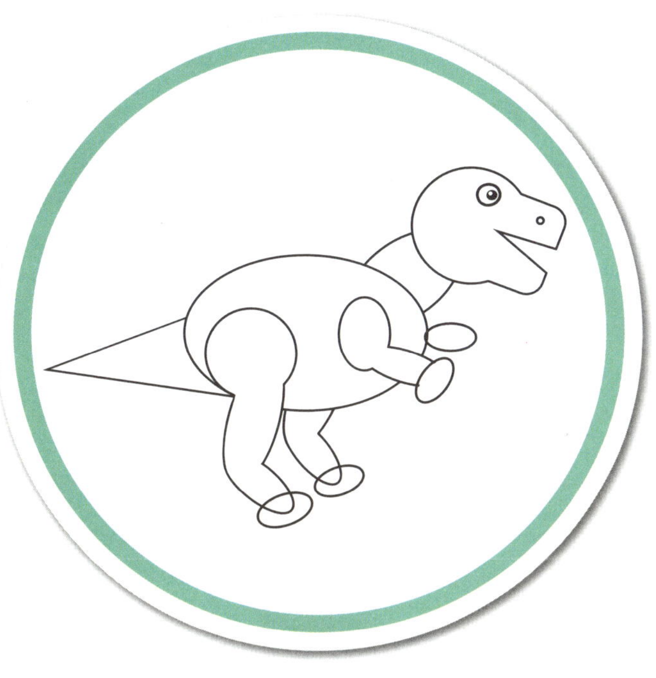

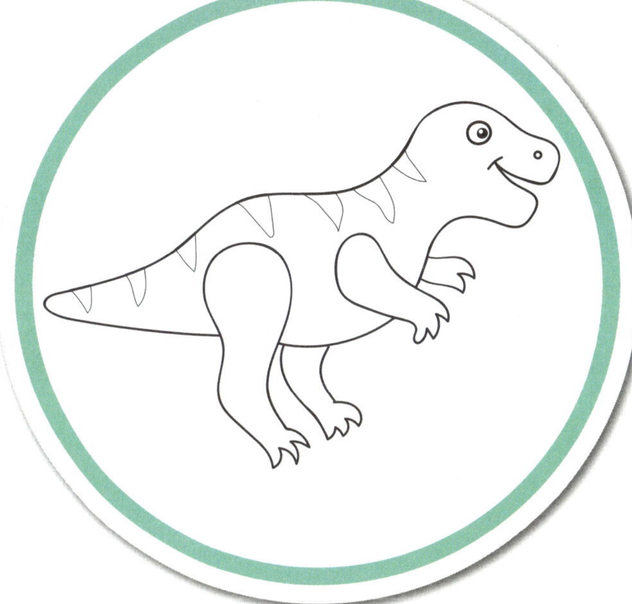

4 Draw fingers and toes on the circles. Draw triangular stripes. Colour to complete.

3 Draw an eye, a nose, a mouth and circles for toes and fingers.

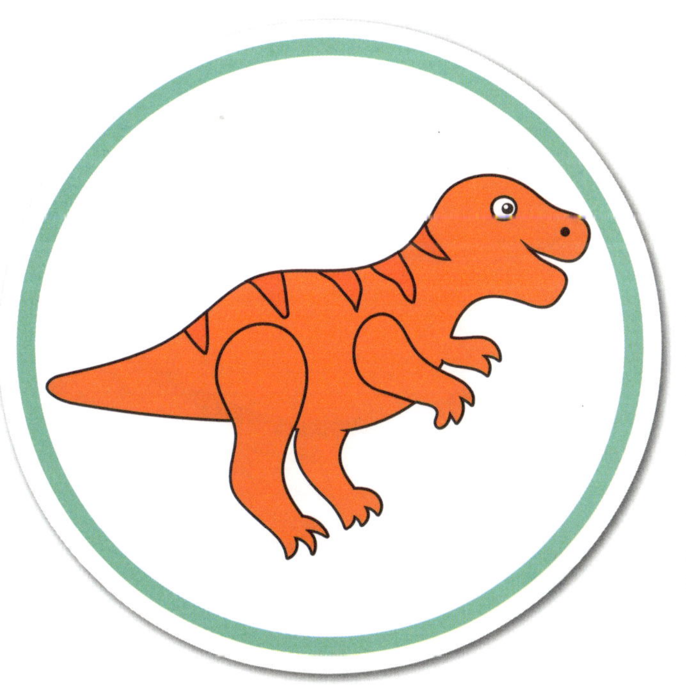

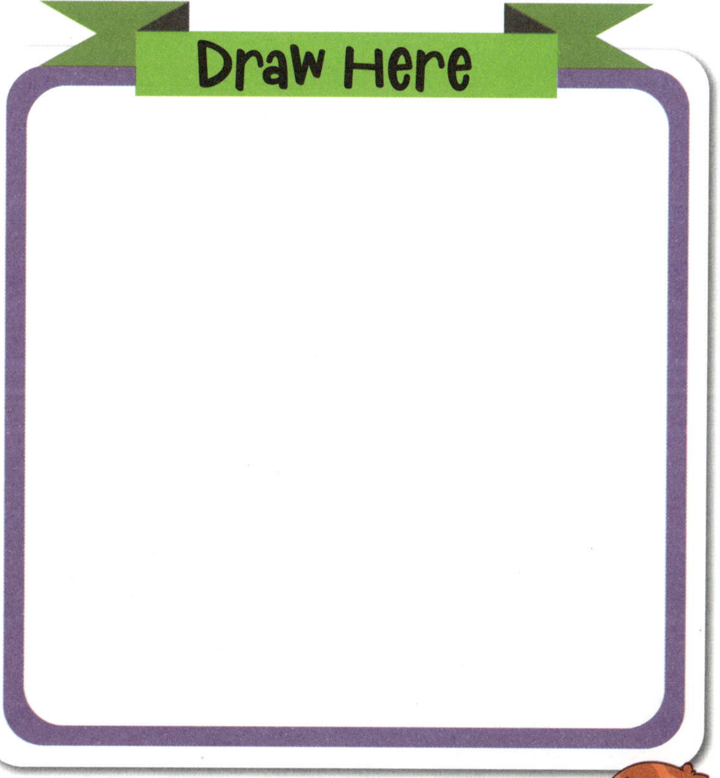

MOSASAURUS

This is Mosasaurus. It is closely related to snakes and monitor lizards.

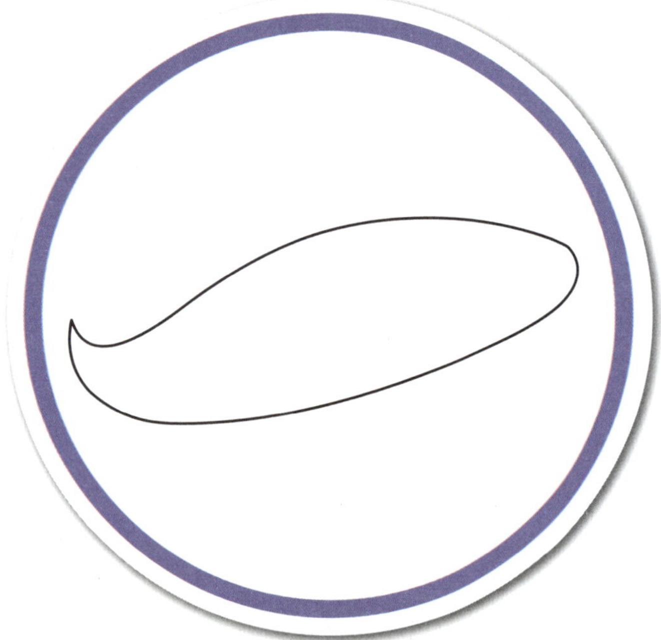

1 Draw an oval shape and curve it at the left end to make a tail.

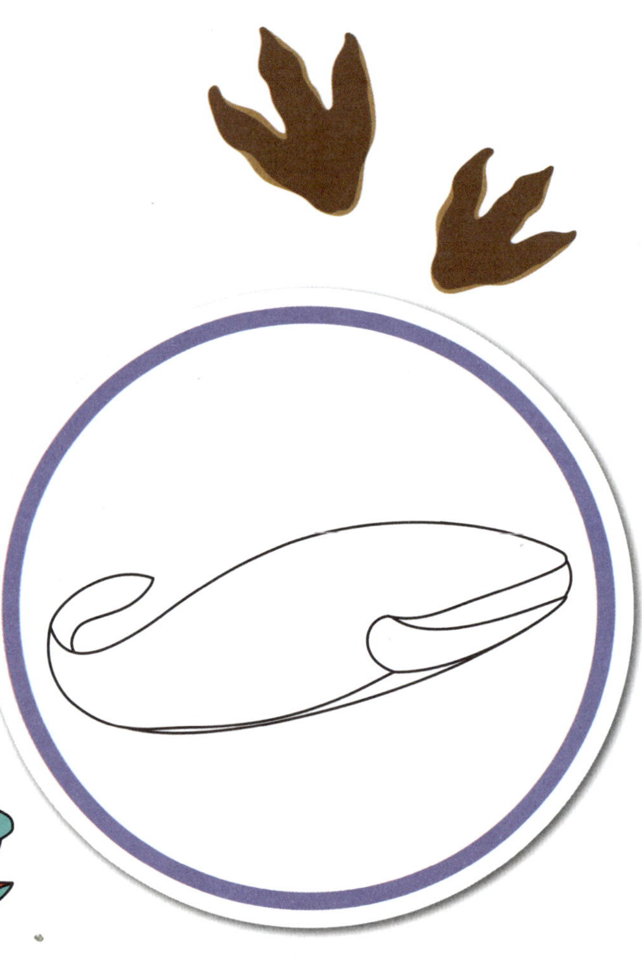

2 Outline it to give shape to the face, body and tail.

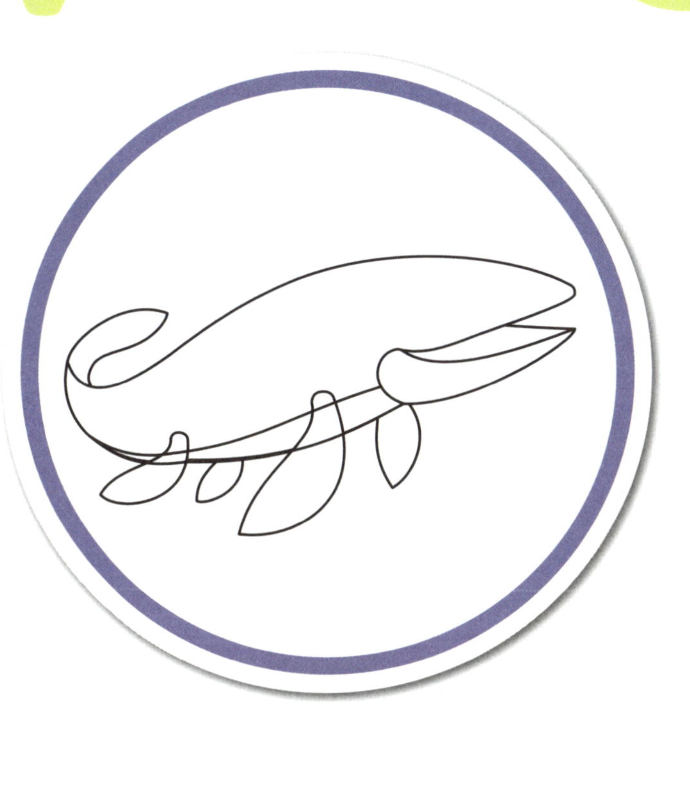

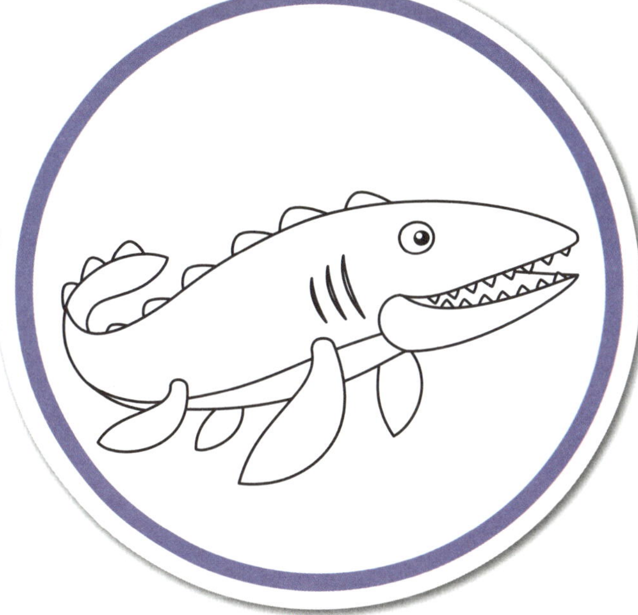

4 Draw an eye, scales, gills and teeth. Colour to complete.

3 Draw four fins at the bottom.

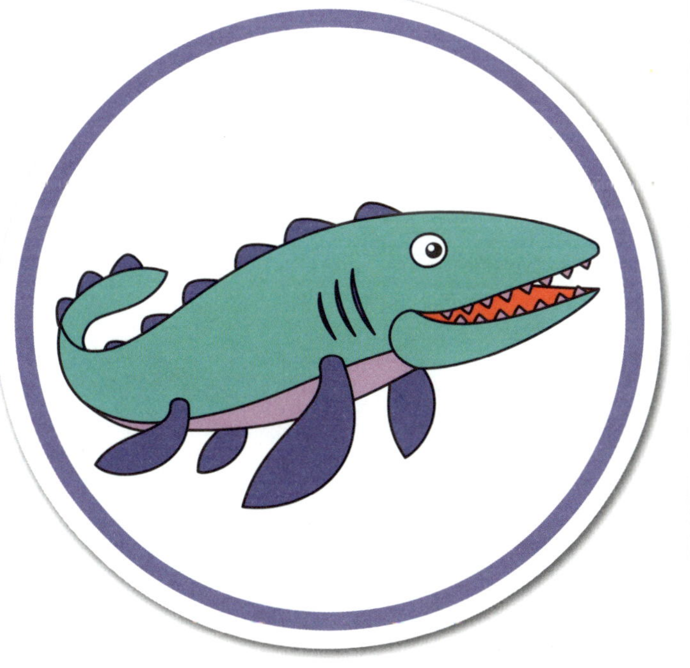

Draw Here

BRACHIOSAURUS

This is Brachiosaurus. It had an incredibly long neck.

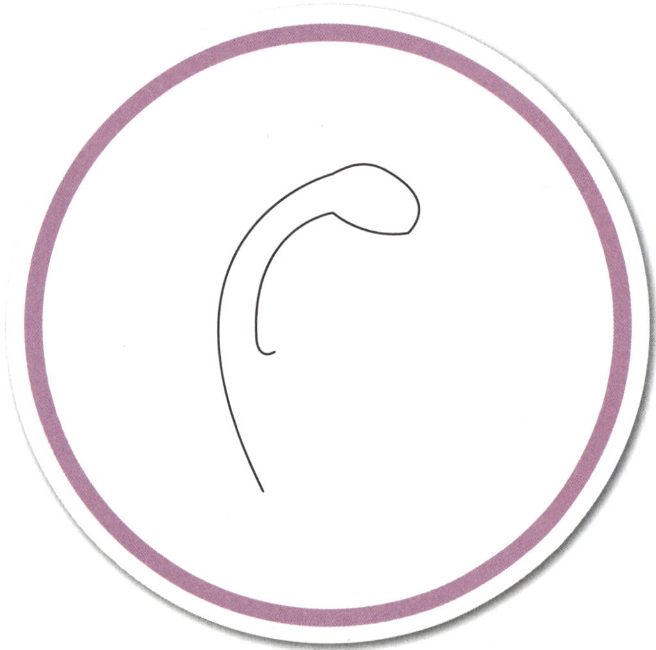

1 Draw the head and then extend two lines downwards for its neck.

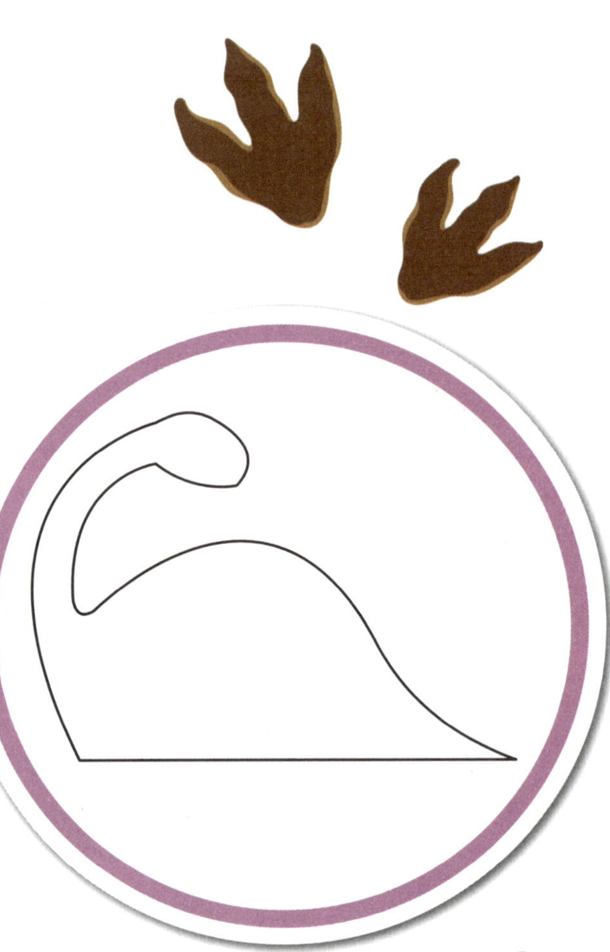

2 Draw the curved shape of a swan and th
draw a straight line at the bottom to mal
the body.

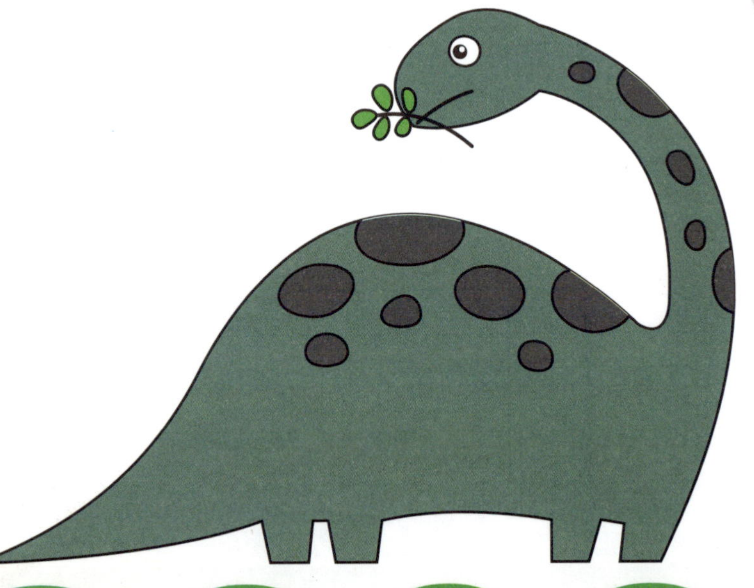

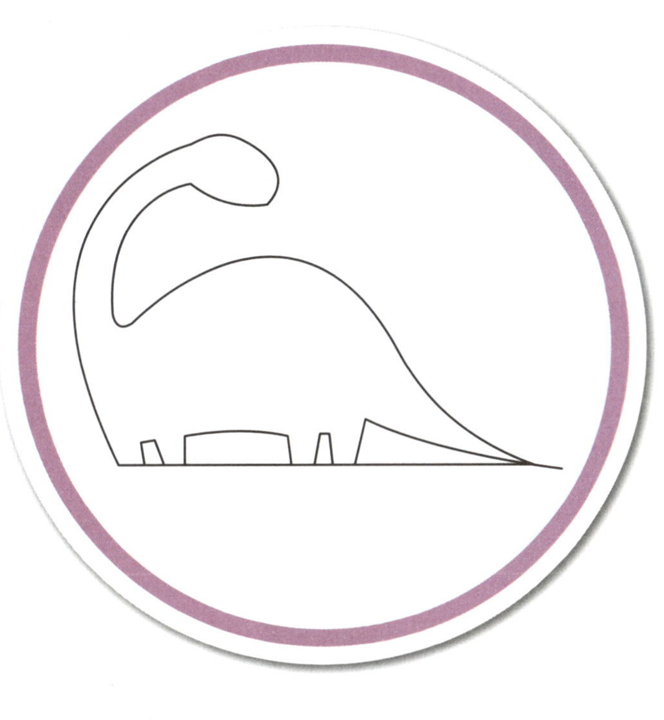

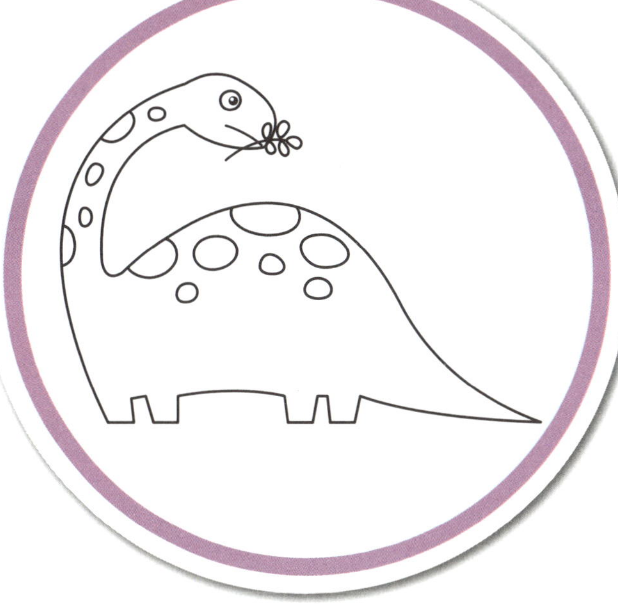

4 Draw the eye, mouth, spots on the body and leaves in the mouth. Colour to complete.

3 Draw legs and a curve at the end to make a tail.

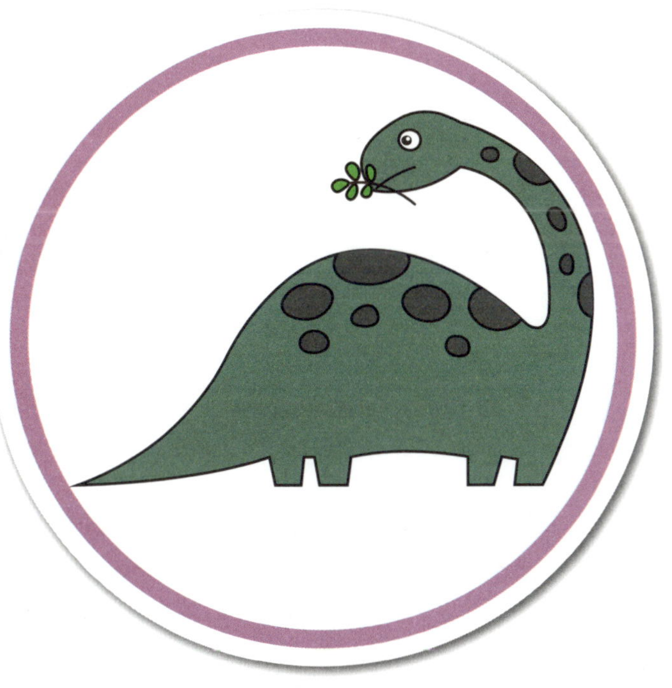

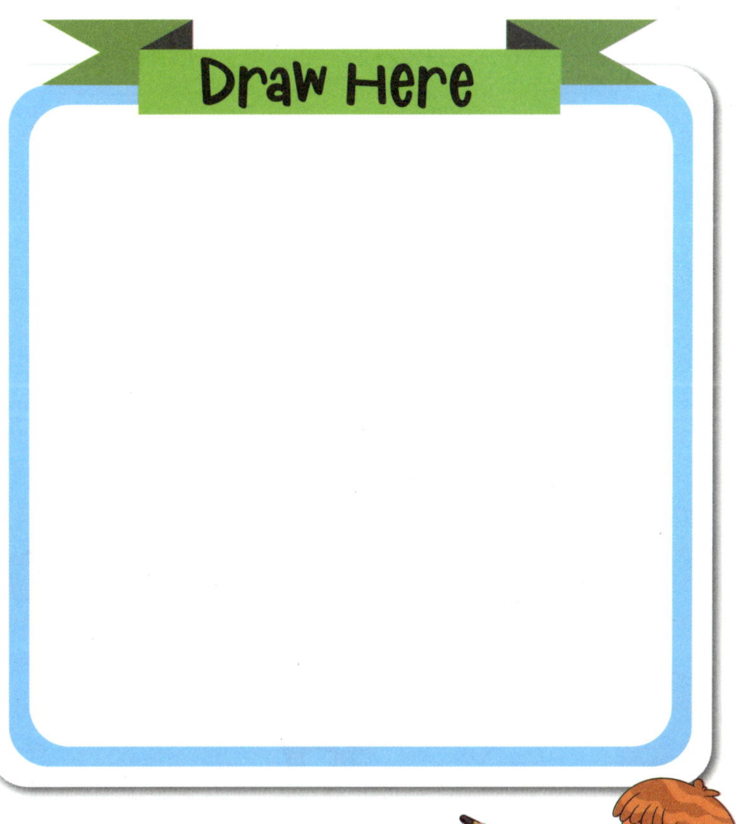

PTEROSAUR

This is a pterosaur. Pterosaurs were flying reptiles who were cousins of dinosaurs.

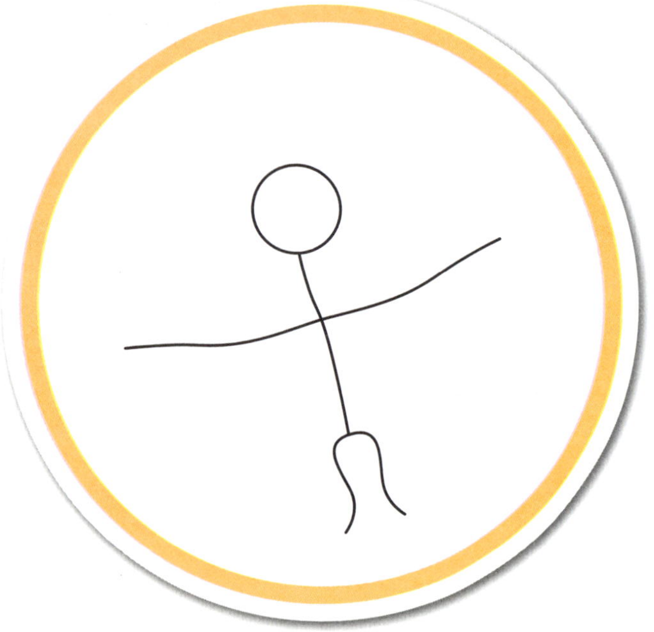

1 Draw a circle for the head. Draw lines for the body, hand and legs.

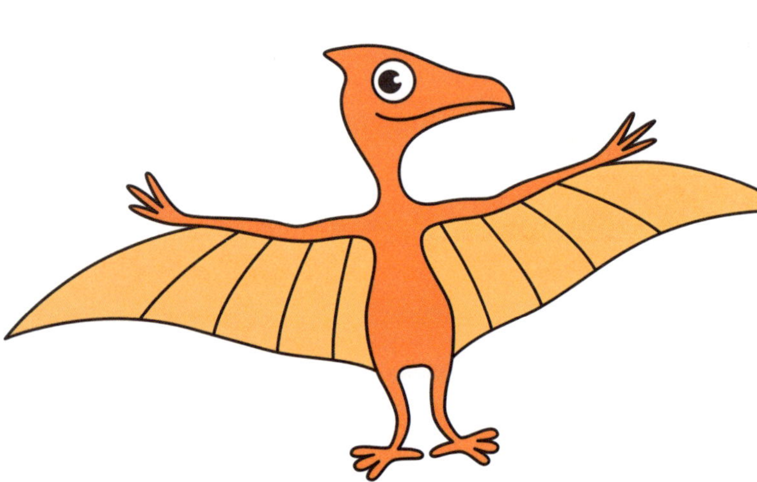

2 Draw an eye and curves to give a definite shape to the pterosaur. Below the arms, make a curved line for the wings.

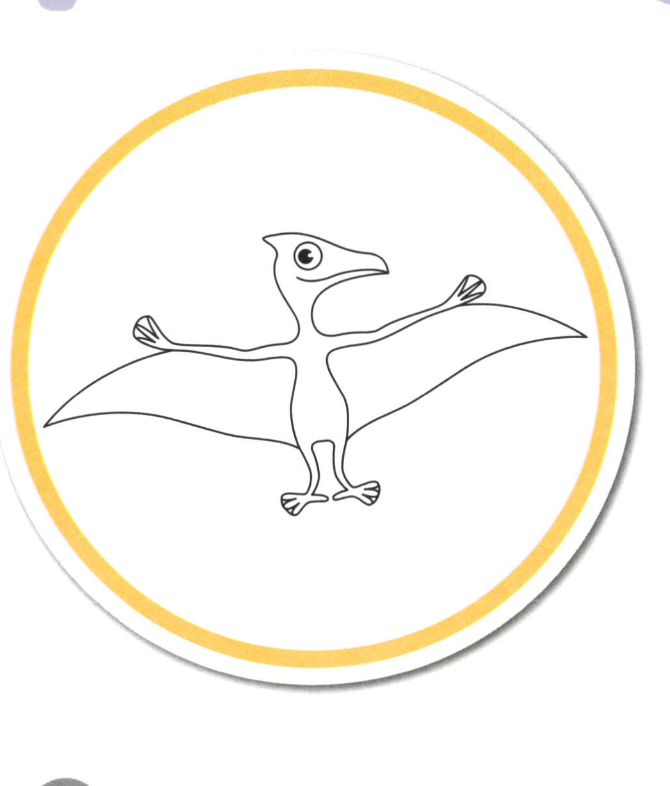

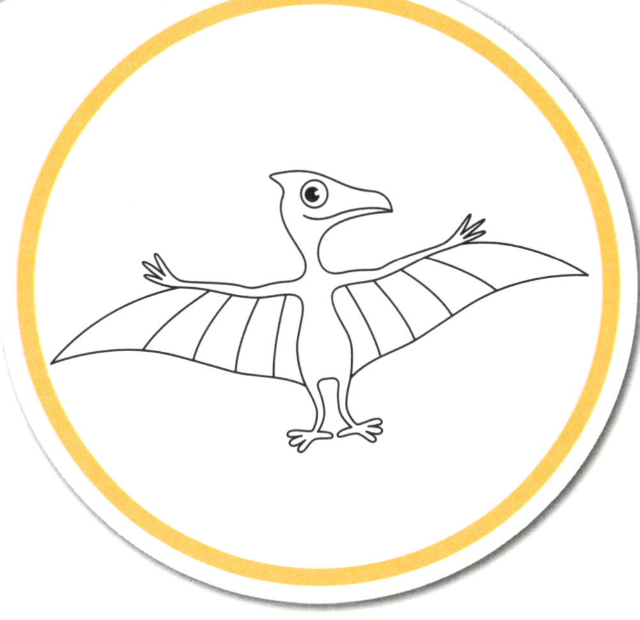

4 Draw lines on the wings.
Colour to complete.

3 Draw wings, fingers and feet.

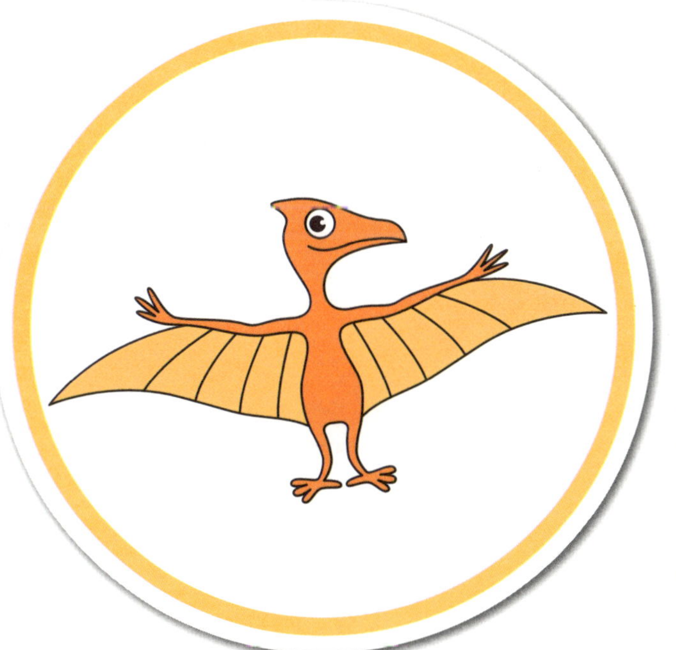

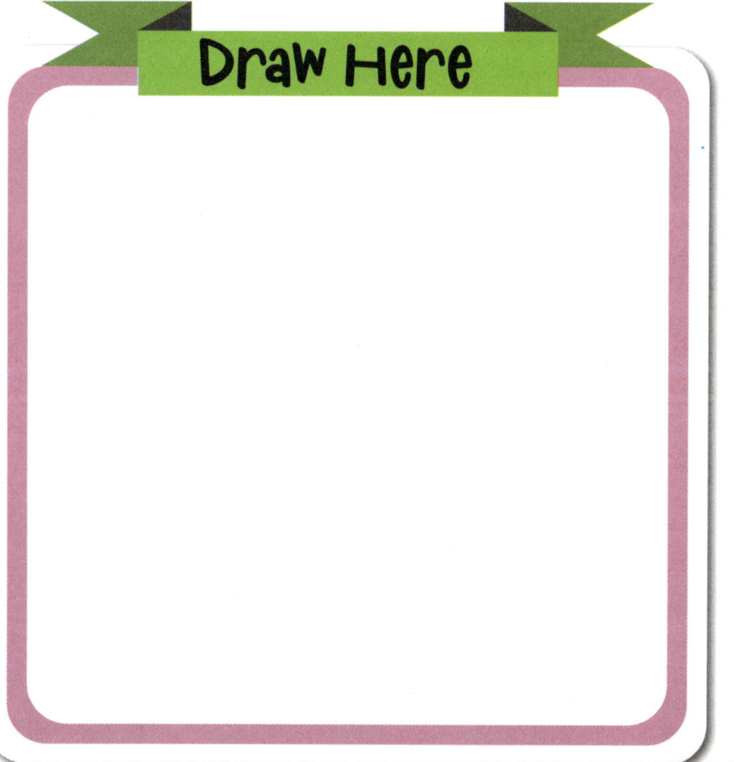

ANKYLOSAURUS

This is Ankylosaurus. It had spikes on its head and body.

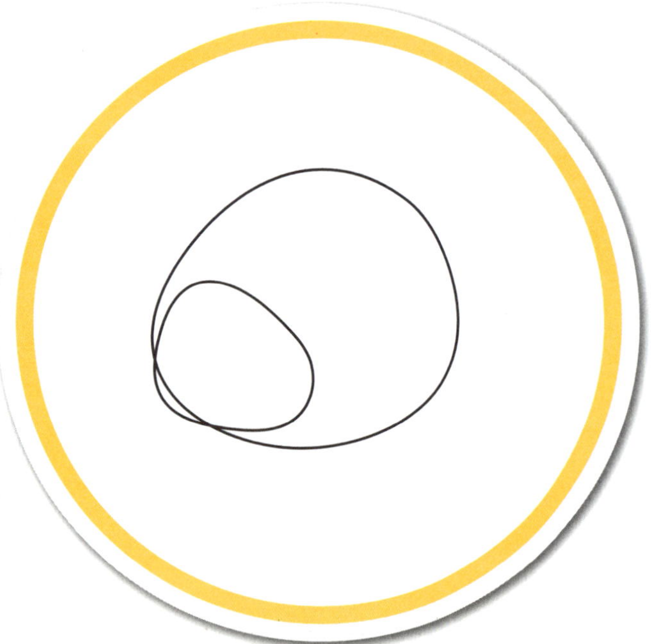

1 Draw a big egg shape for the body and inside it, draw another shape for the head.

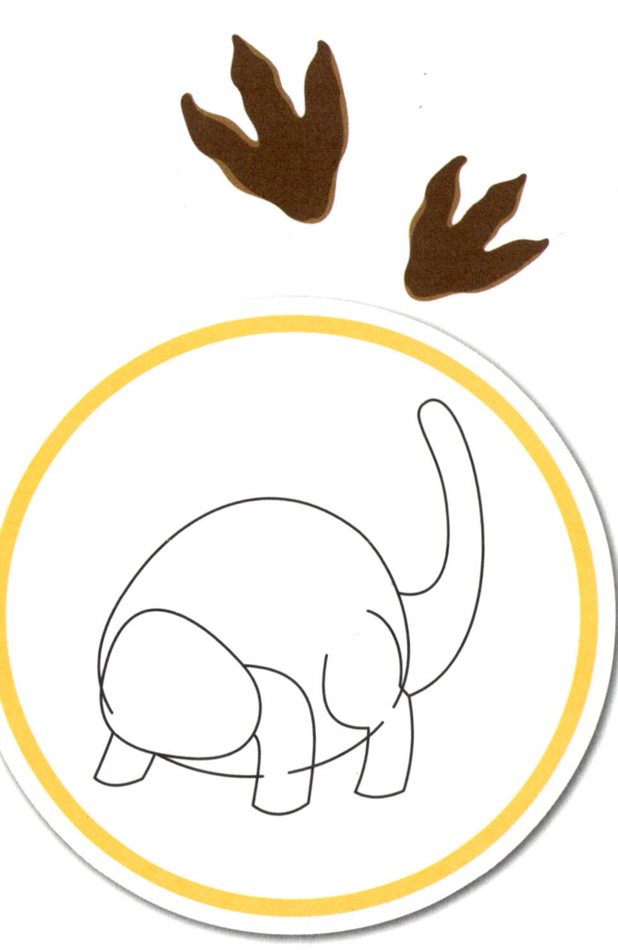

2 Draw a tail, front and hind legs. Erase unwanted lines.

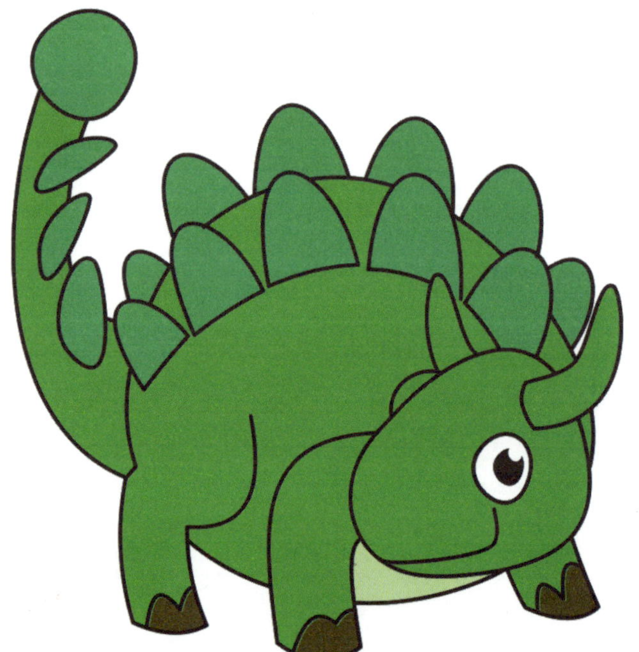

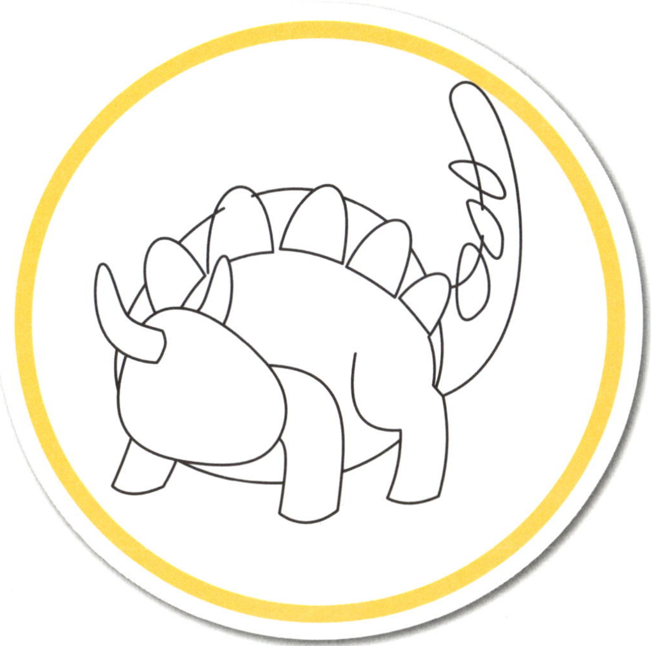

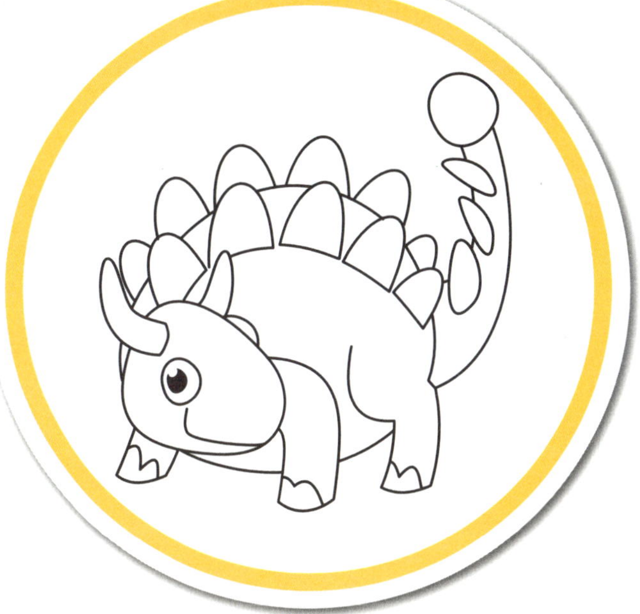

4 Draw an eye and fill it in too. Make a mouth. Colour to complete.

3 Draw horns. Draw a double outline as the body. On that line, make spikes on the inside and outer sides of the body.

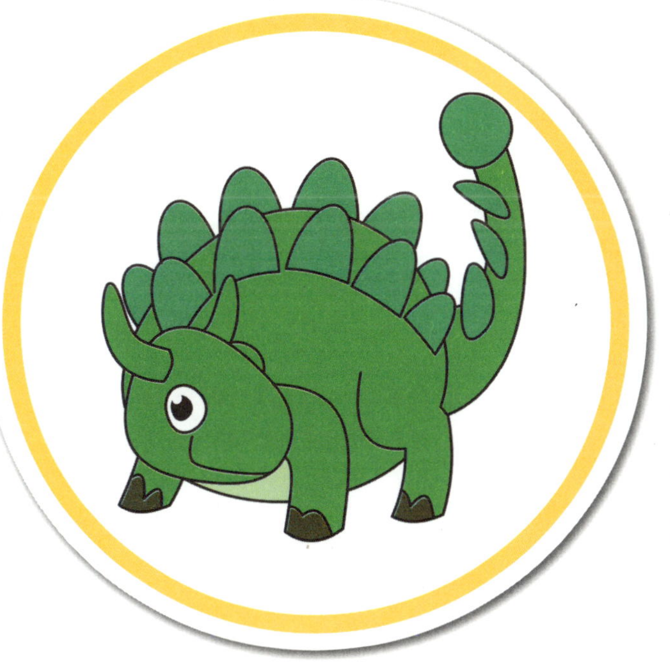

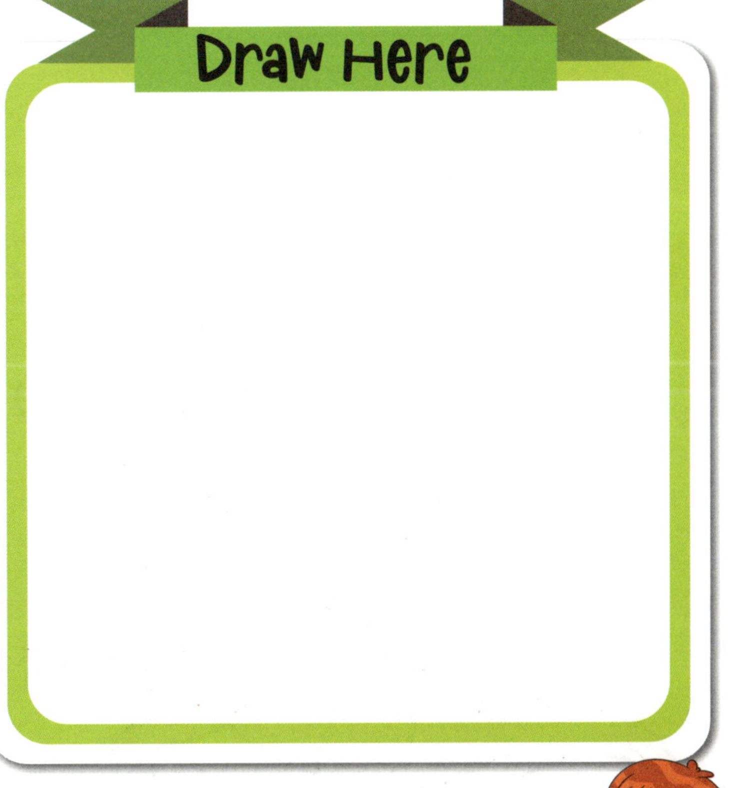

IGUANODON

This is Iguanodon. It was a large, bulky herbivore, measuring up to 36 feet.

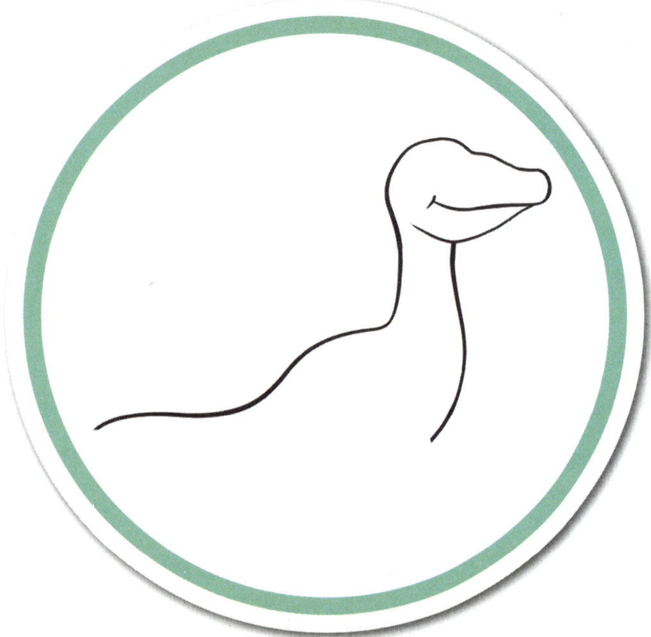

1 Draw an egg shape and curve it to make a face. Draw the body and mouth.

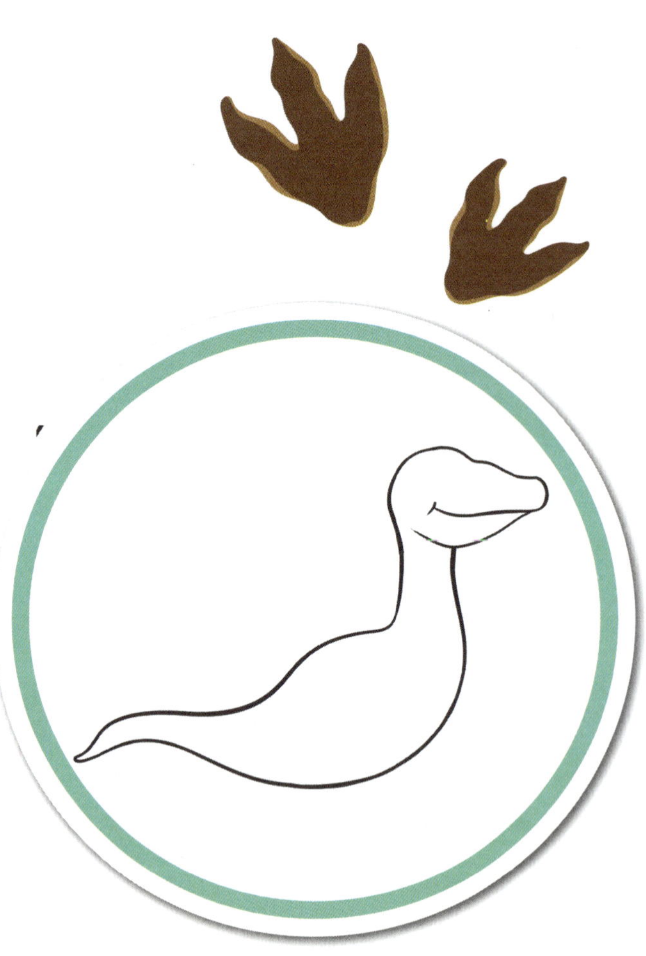

2 Join the lower body with the upper body.

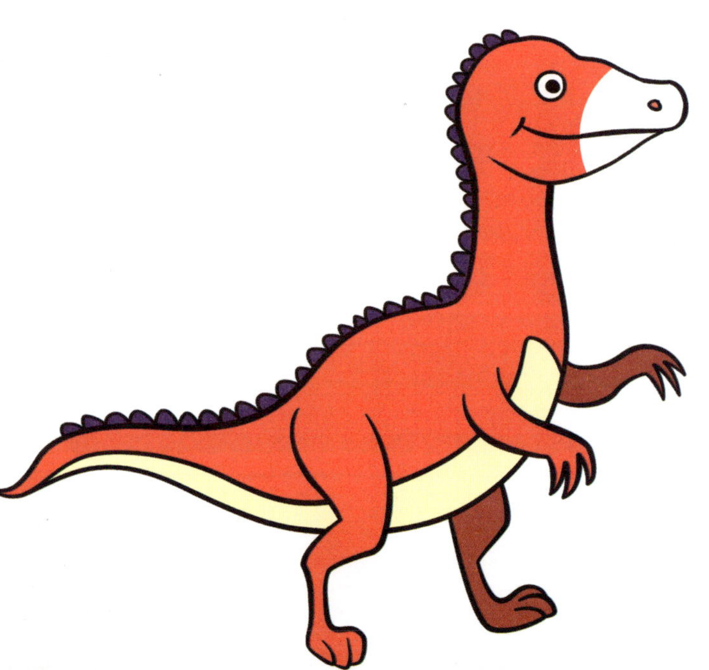

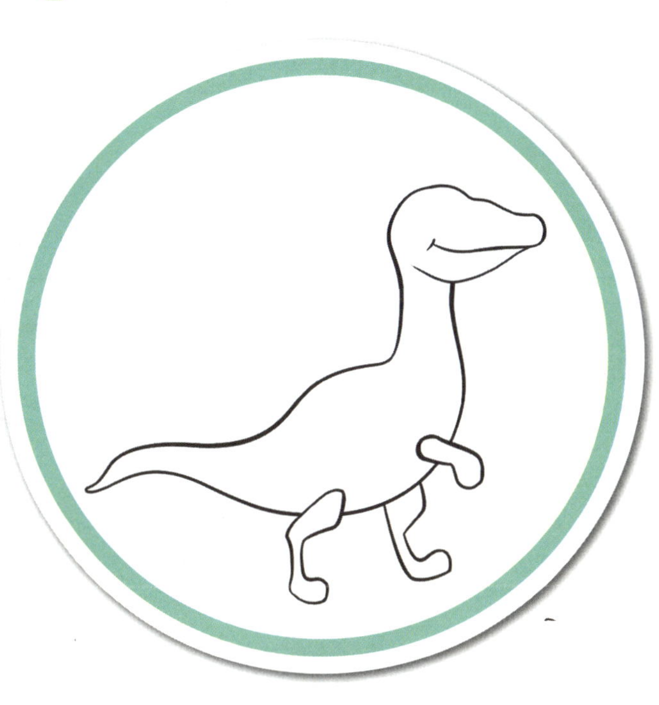

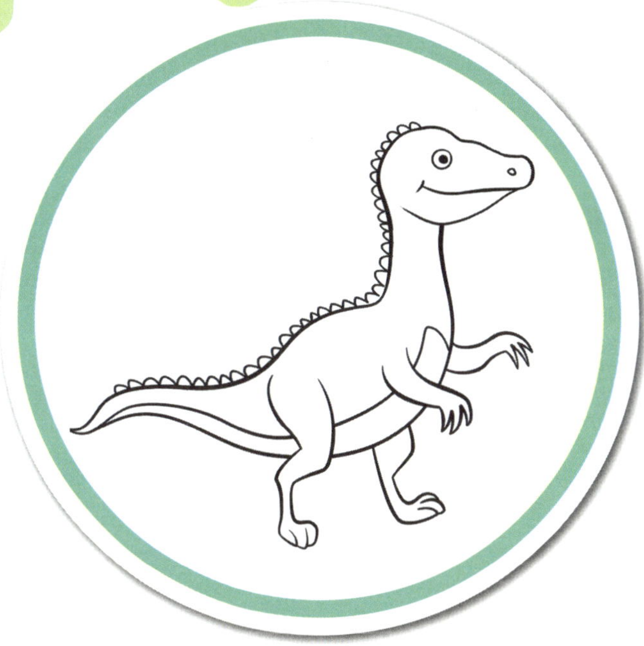

4 Draw curved, tiny spikes on the back. Draw an eye and an arm. Draw a line to make the lower body. Colour to complete.

3 Draw an arm and legs.

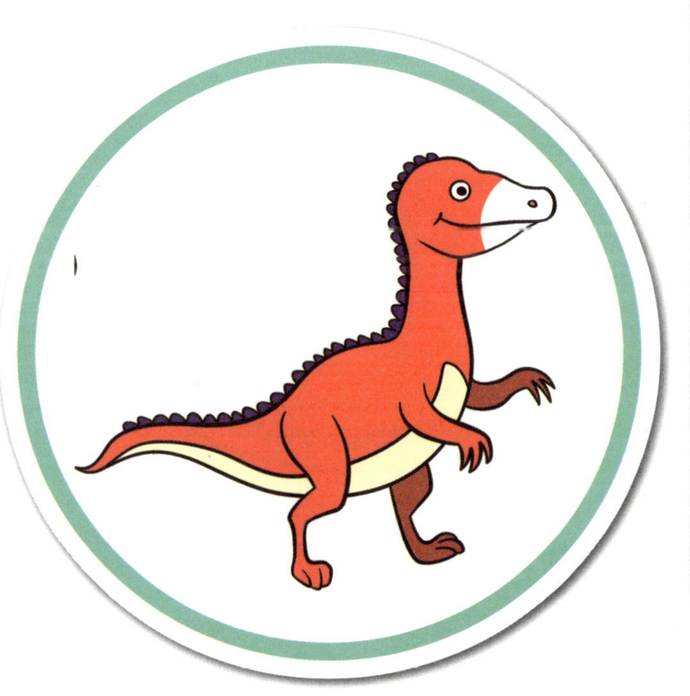

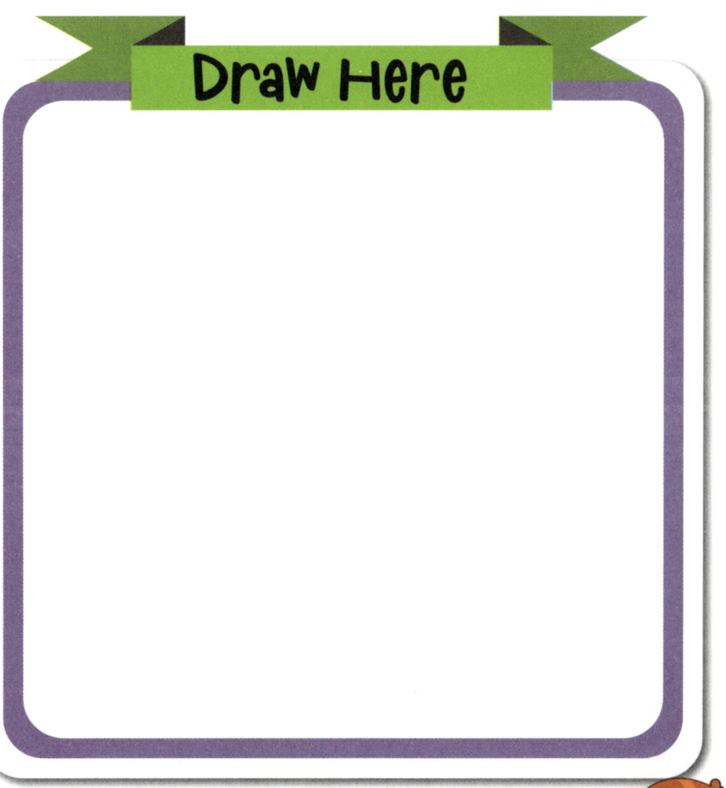

GALLIMIMUS

This is Gallimimus. It could run at a speed of around 80 kph.

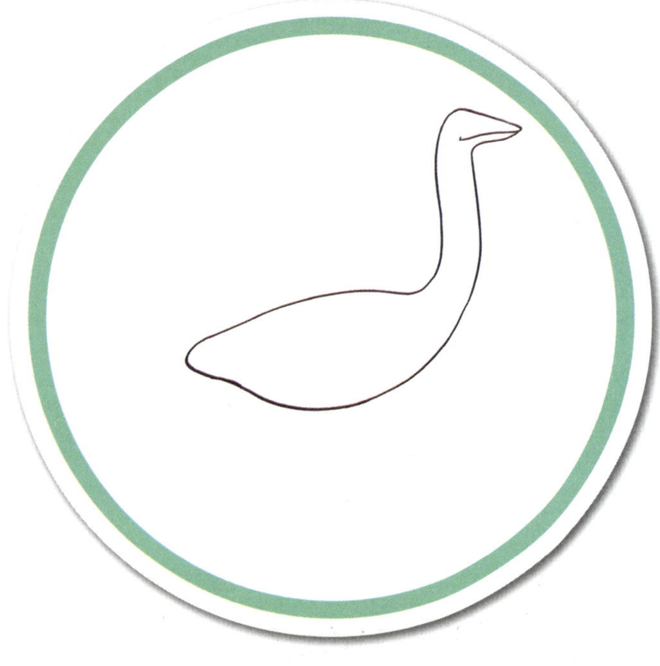

1 Draw the shape of a swan and a line on the face for the mouth.

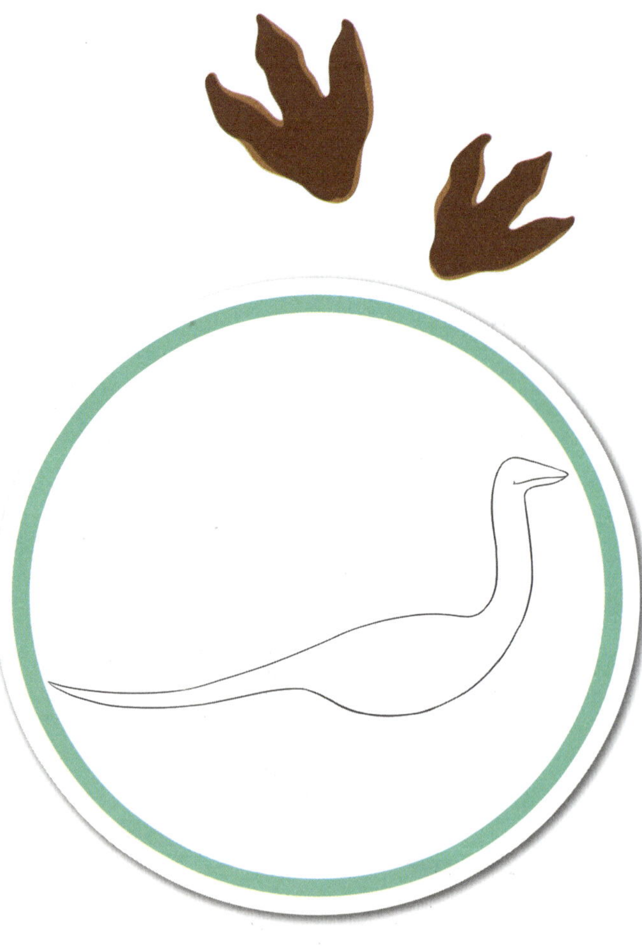

2 Extend the end of the body to form the tail.

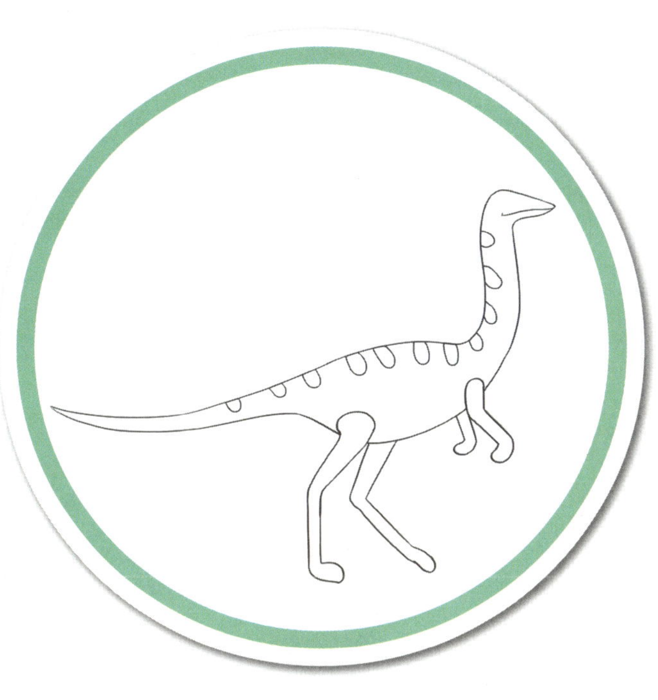

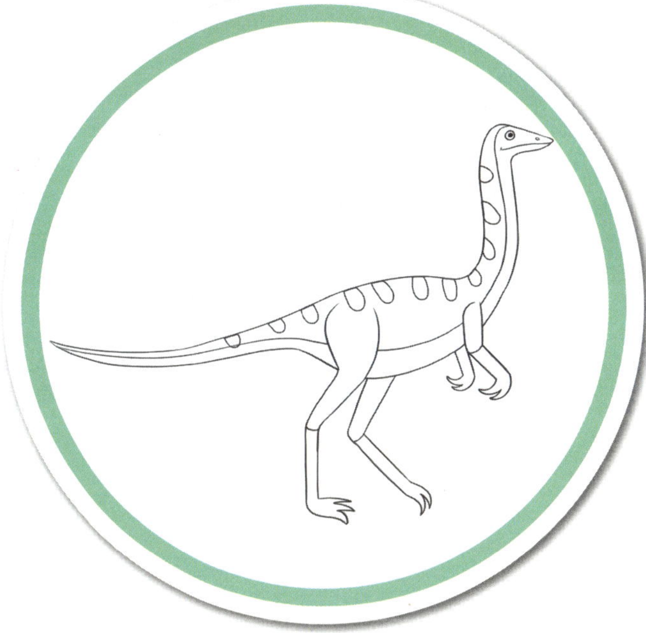

4 Draw the eye. Draw toes and a line from the face to the lower body. Colour to complete.

3 Draw arms and legs. Draw spots touching the upper body.

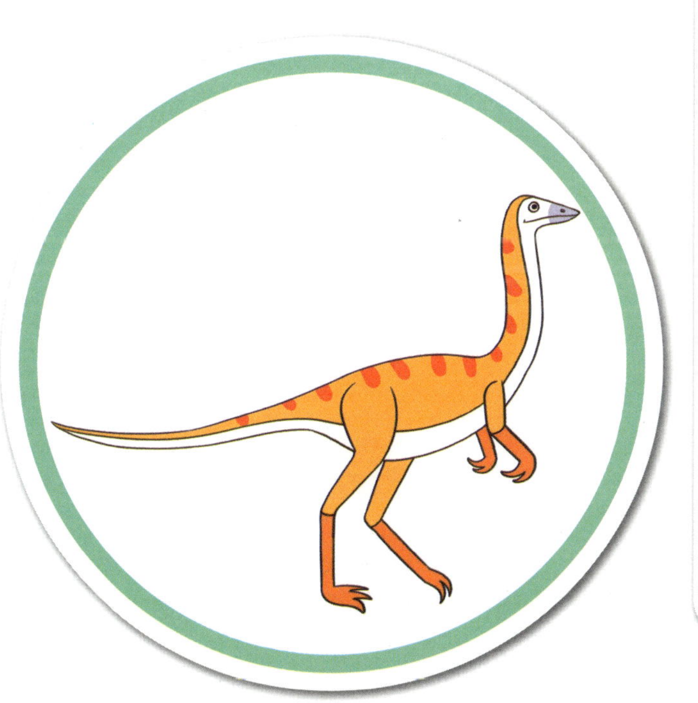

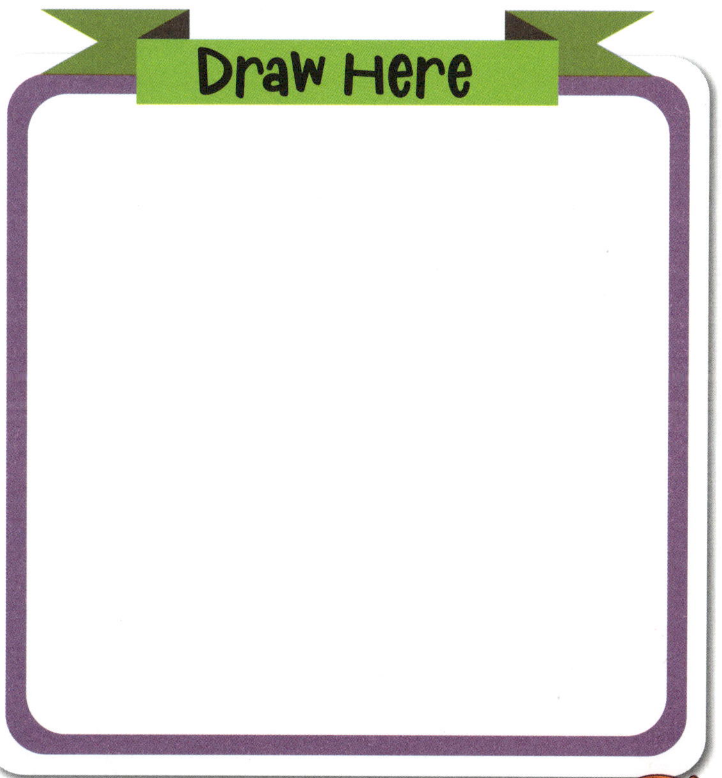

ANDESAURUS

This is Andesaurus. It was a herbivore. It lived in the Cretaceous period.

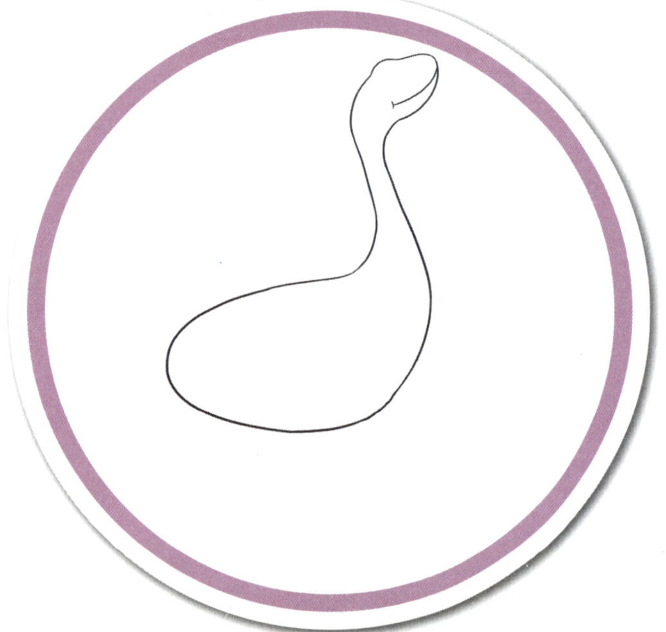

1 Draw an egg shape, then erase the end and stretch it up to make a neck and head.

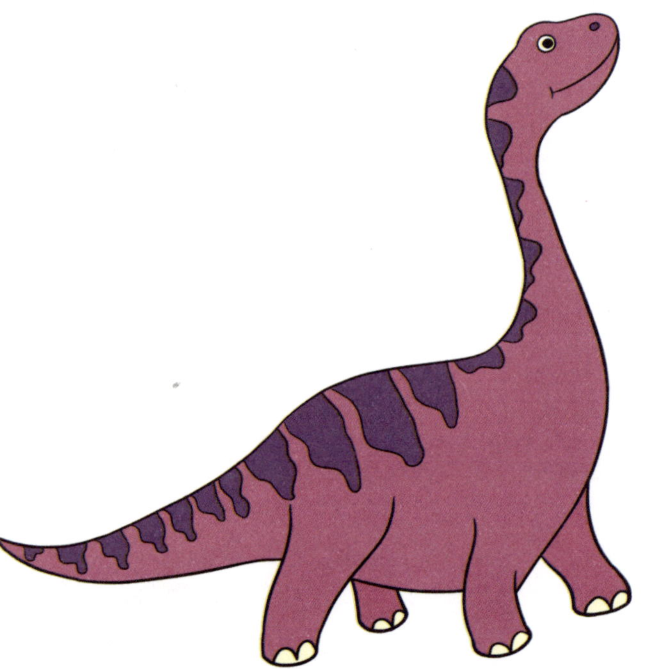

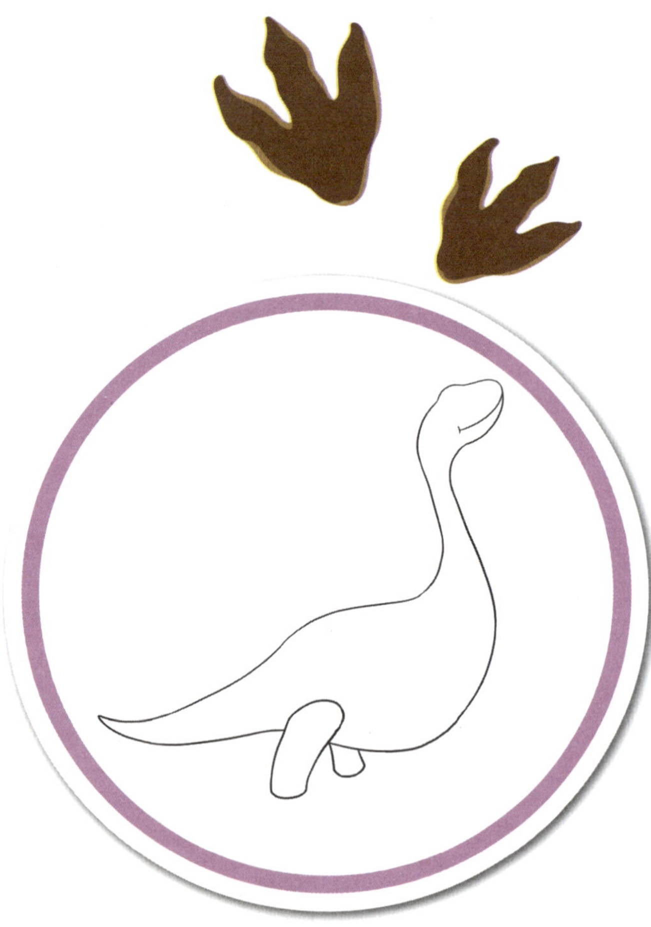

2 Erase the lower end of the body to make a tail. Draw two legs.

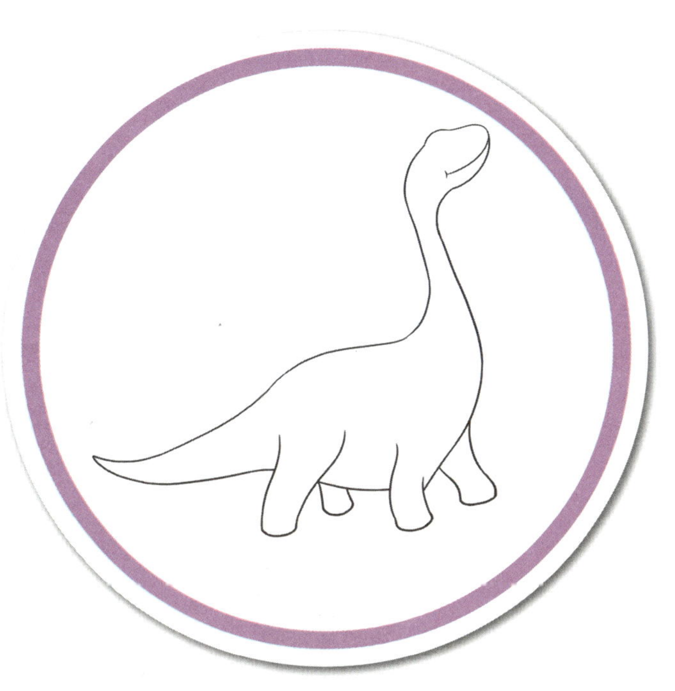

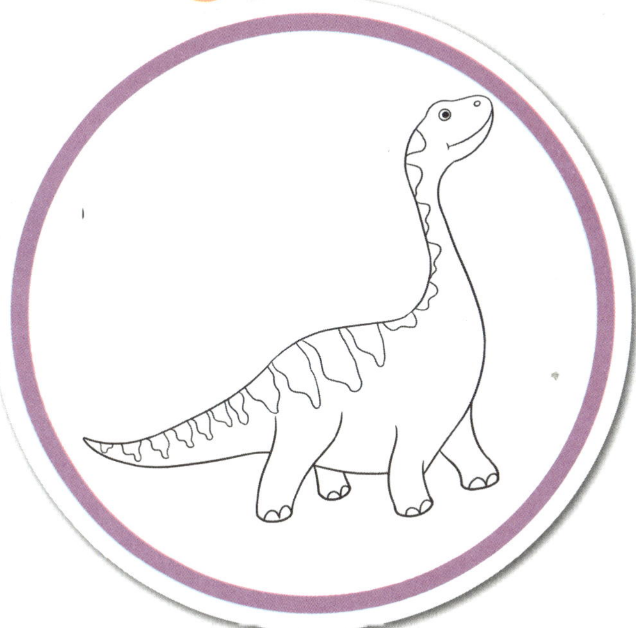

4 Draw the eye, nostril and zigzag stripes. Draw toes on the feet. Colour to complete.

3 Draw the remaining two legs.

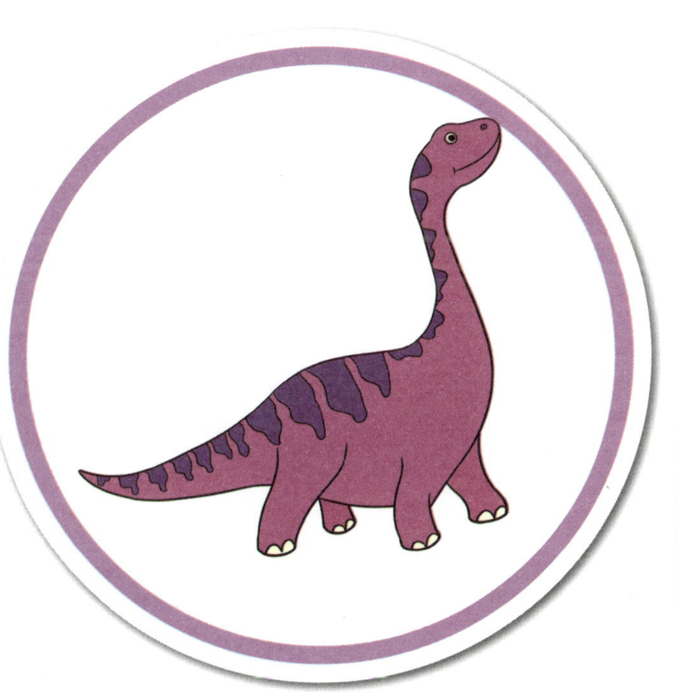

Draw Here

LIRAINOSAURUS

This is Lirainosaurus. It lived in the Cretaceous period.

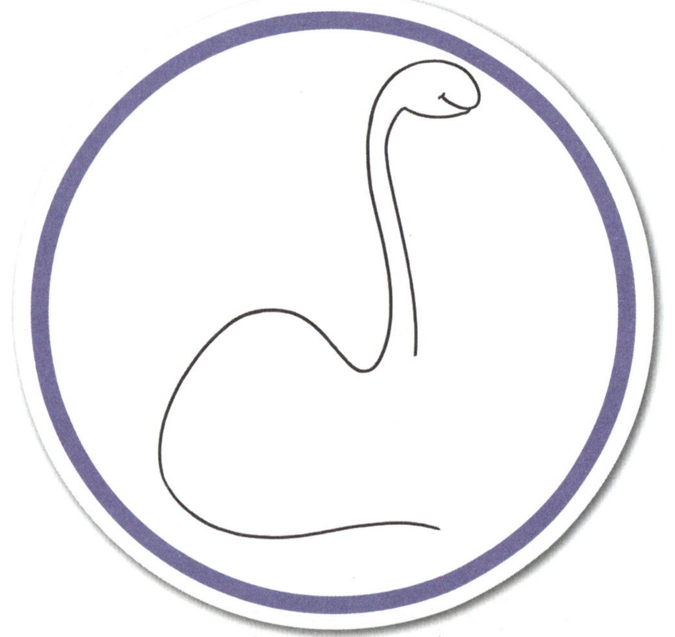

1 Draw a "C" shape. Extend from above to make the neck, face and mouth.

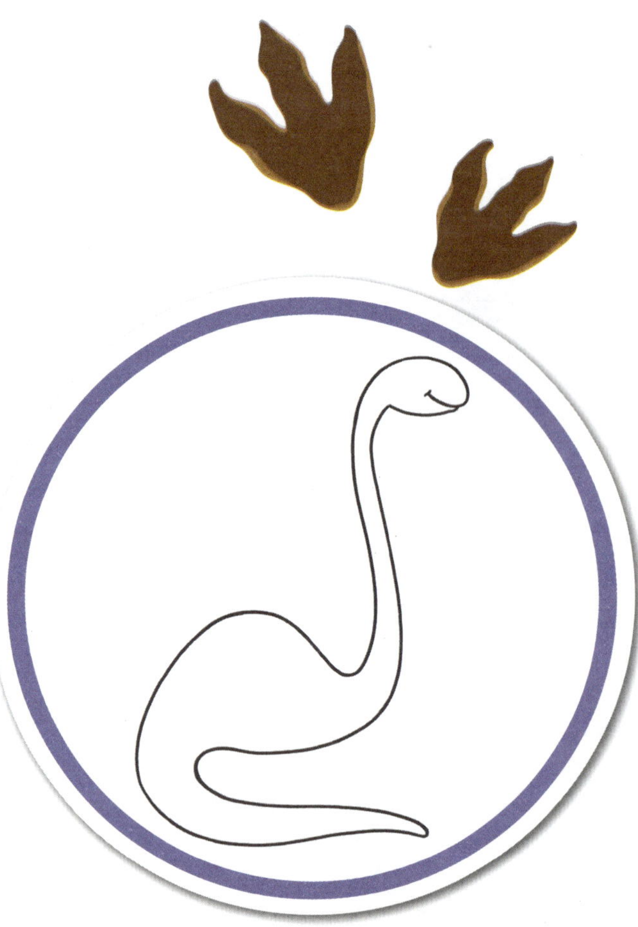

2 From the bottom, extend to make a tail.

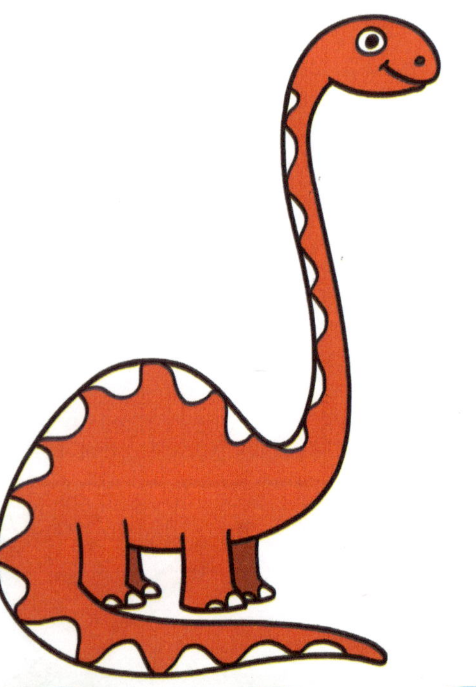

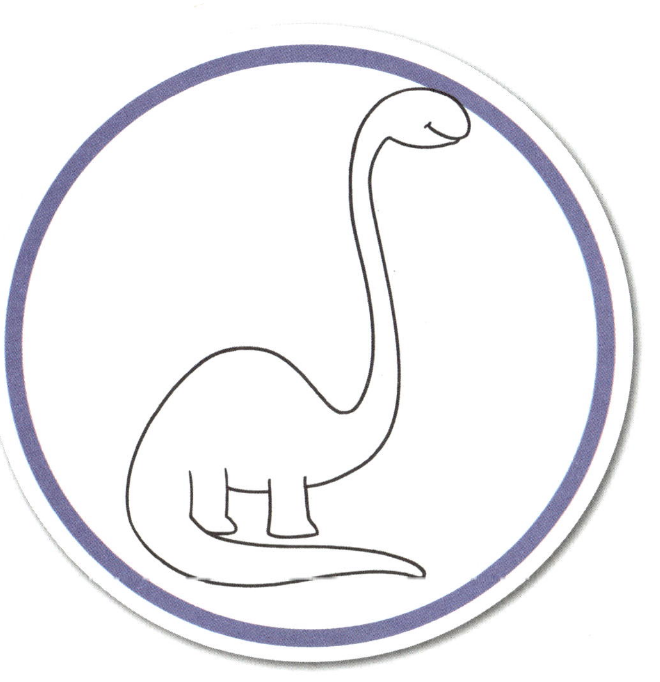

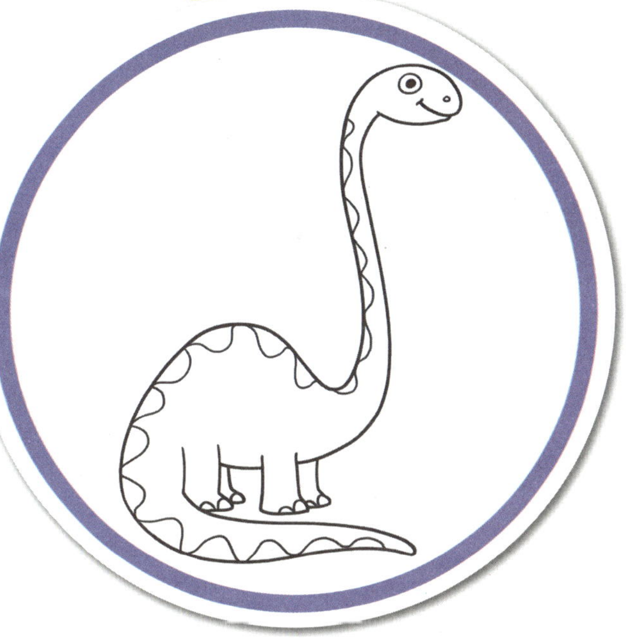

4 Draw a curved design on the body. Draw the remaining legs and toes. Colour to complete.

3 Draw legs from the lower part of the body.

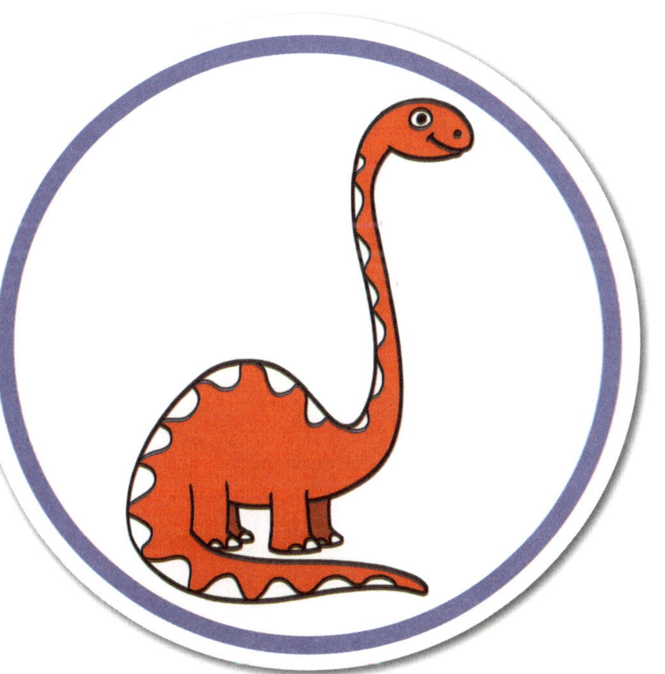

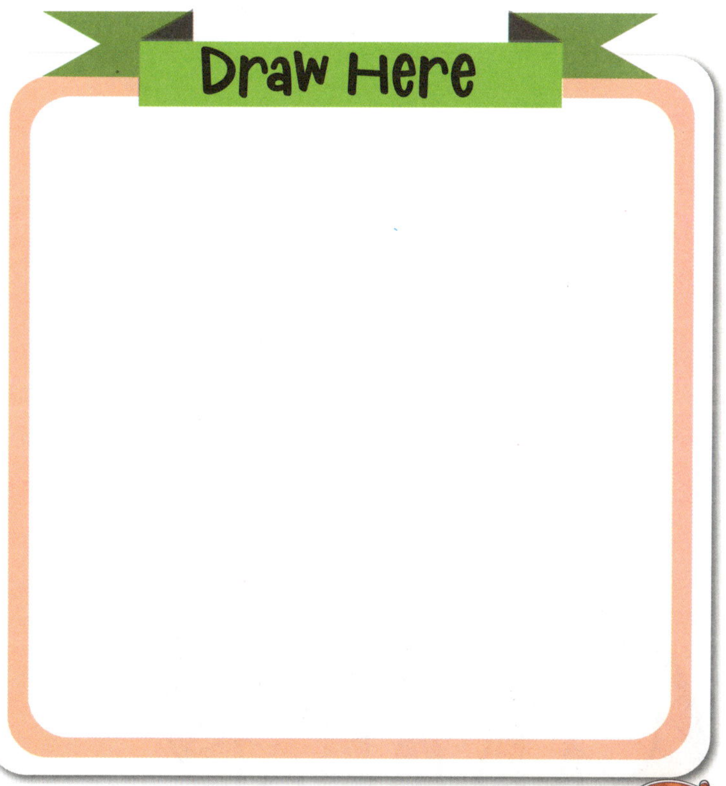

BRONTOSAURUS

This is Brontosaurus. Its name means "Thunder Lizard."

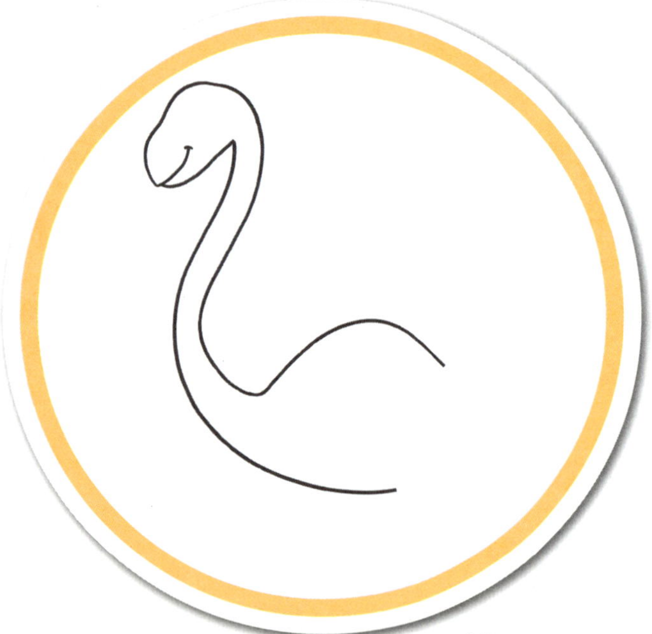

1 Draw the shape of a swan to make the head, neck and body.

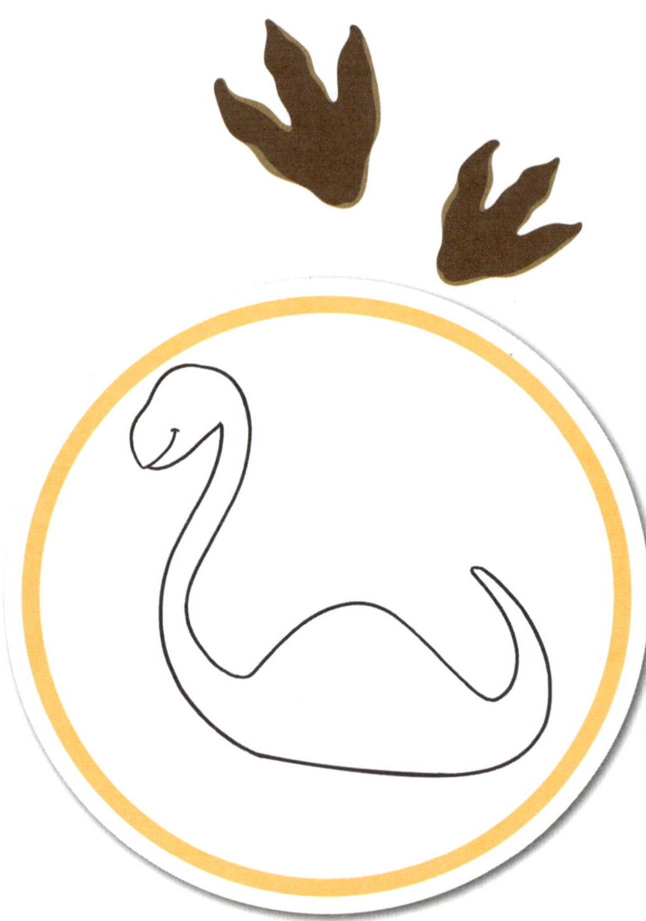

2 Extend the last part to make a tail.

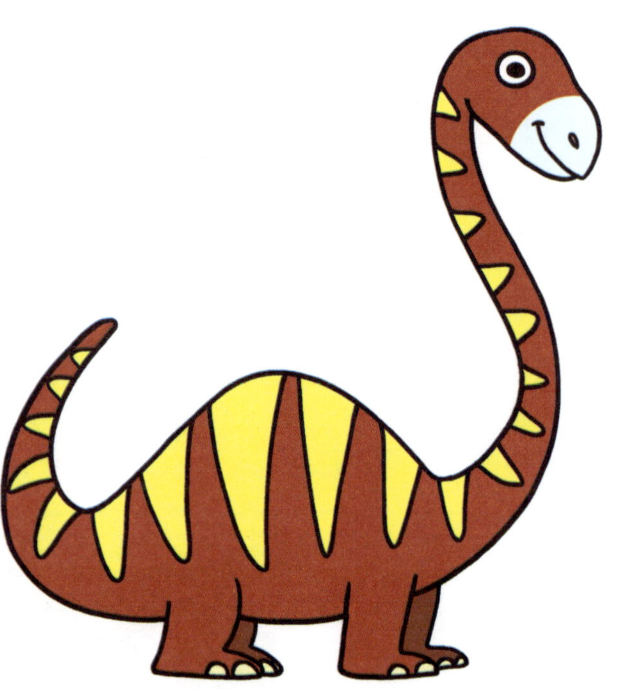

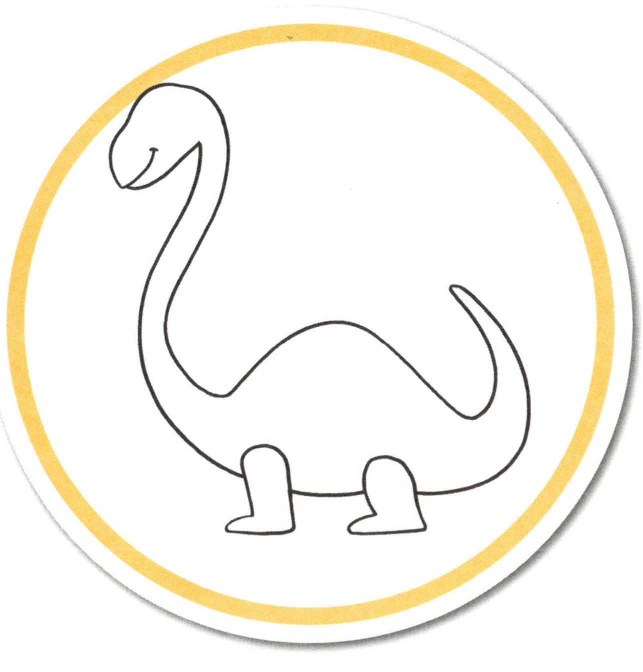

3 Draw legs at the bottom of the body.

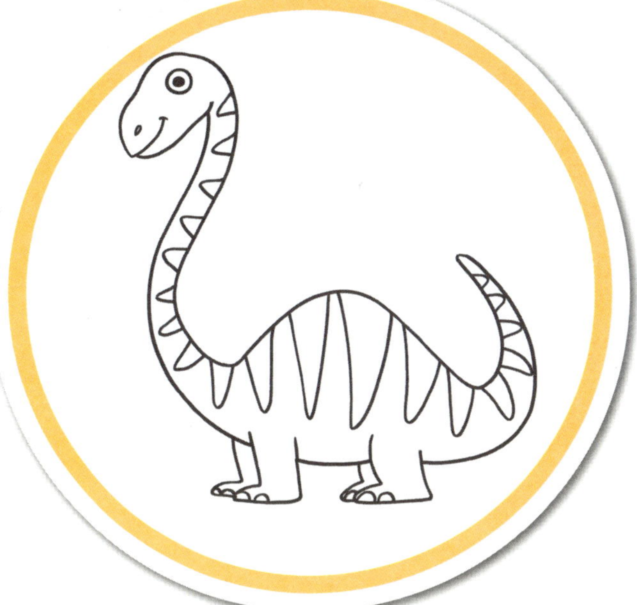

4 Draw the eye, nostril and conical stripes for the body. Draw the remaining legs and toes. Colour to complete.

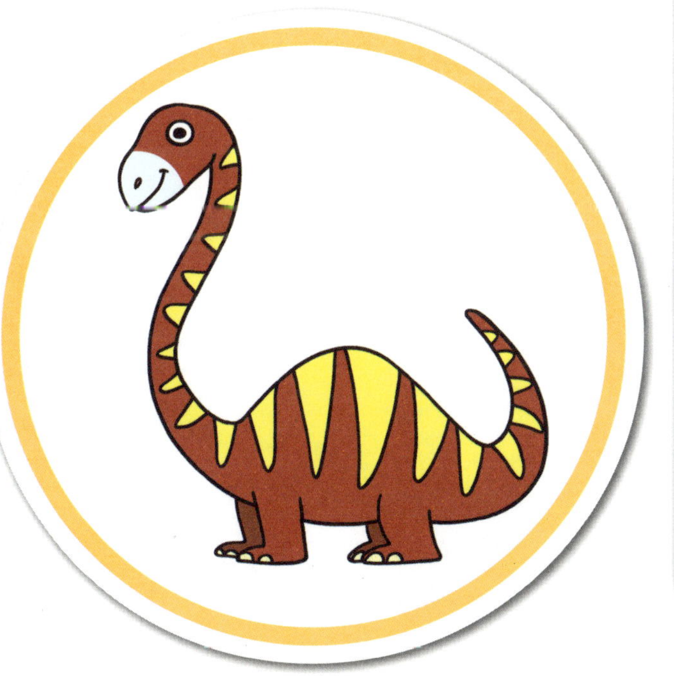

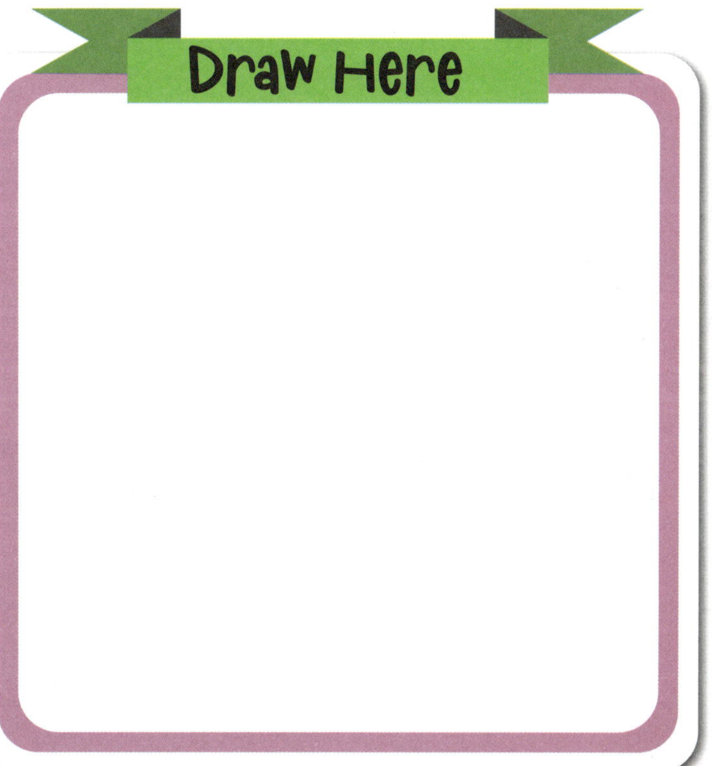

EUROPASAURUS

This is Europasarus. It was one of the smallest known sauropod dinosaurs.

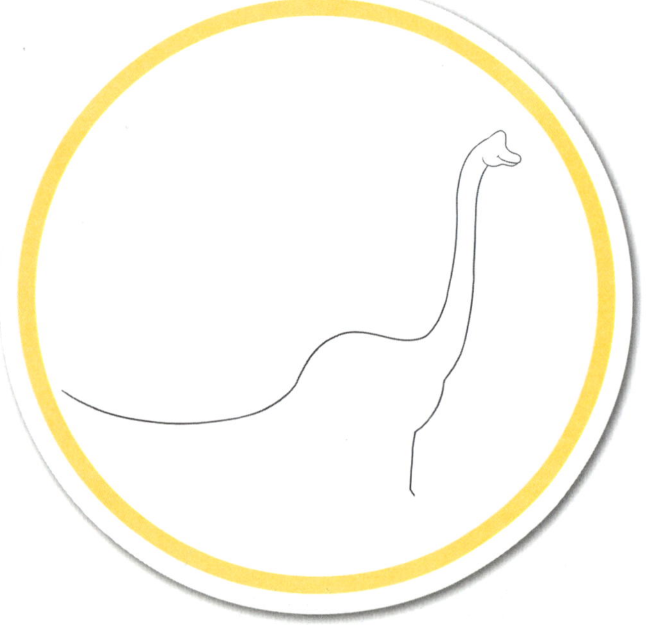

1 Draw the head, mouth, a long neck and the body. Extend the lower part for the tail.

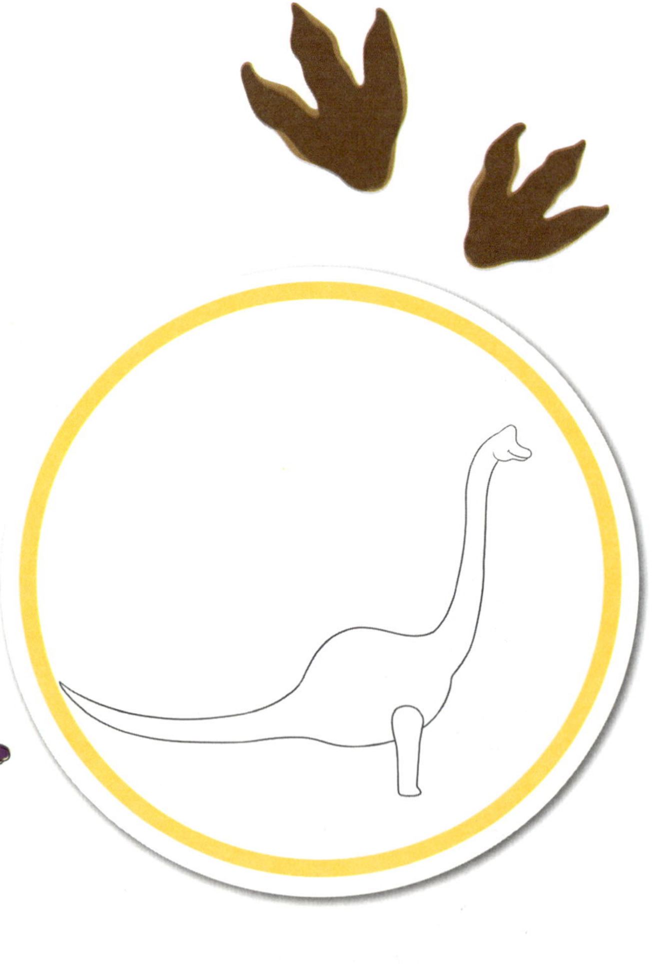

2 Draw the lower part of the body and the leg.

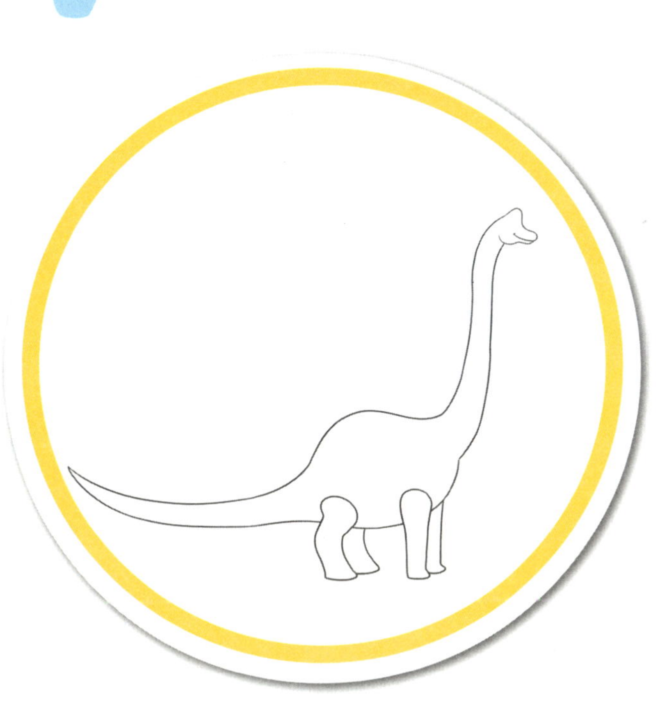

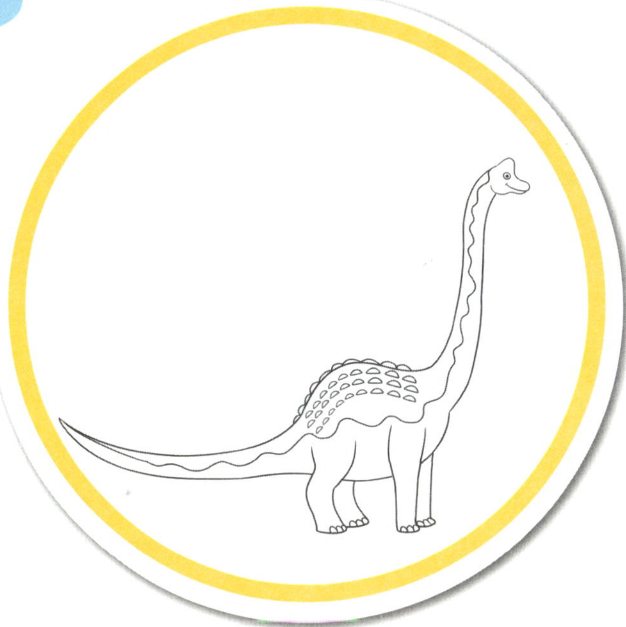

4 Draw designs inside the body of the dinosaur. Draw the eye. Colour to complete.

3 Draw the remaining three legs.

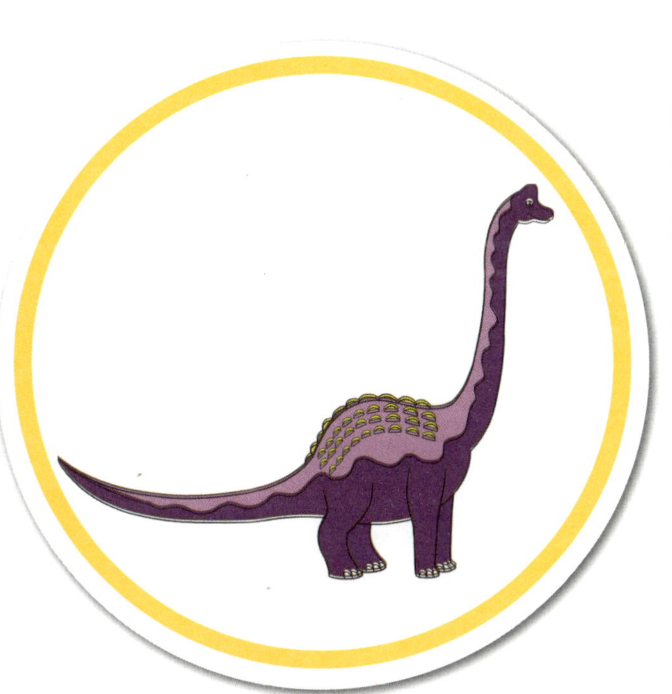

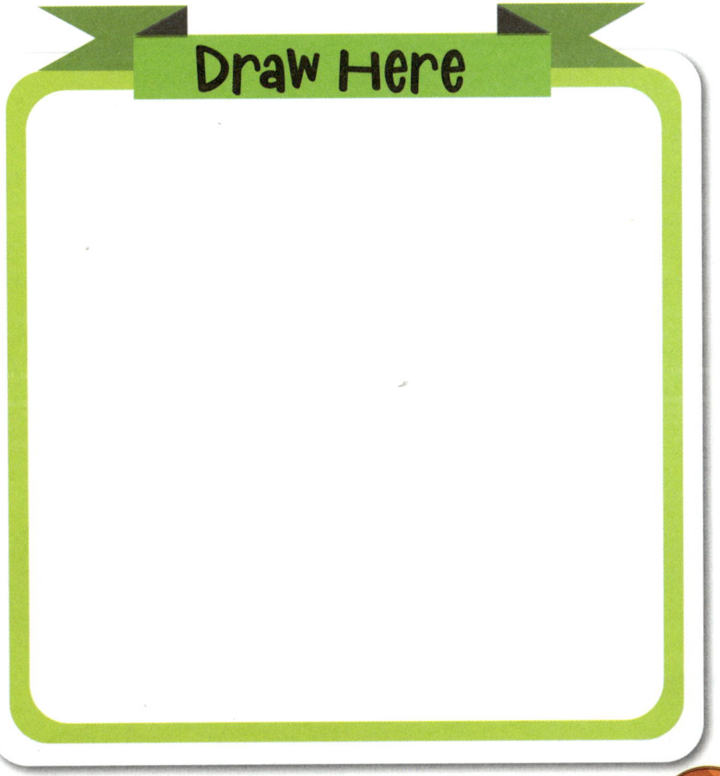

COELOPHYSIS

This is Coelophysis. It had very sharp teeth.

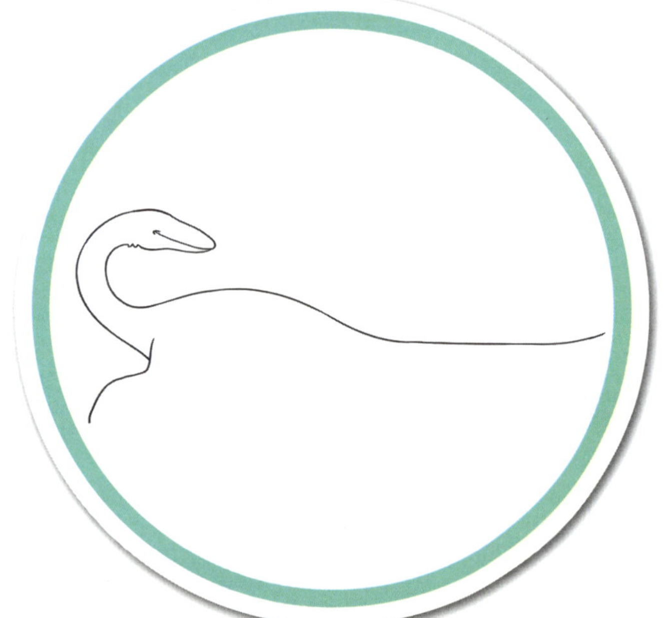

1 Draw a head like that of a snake. Draw a neck and a curved line for the body.

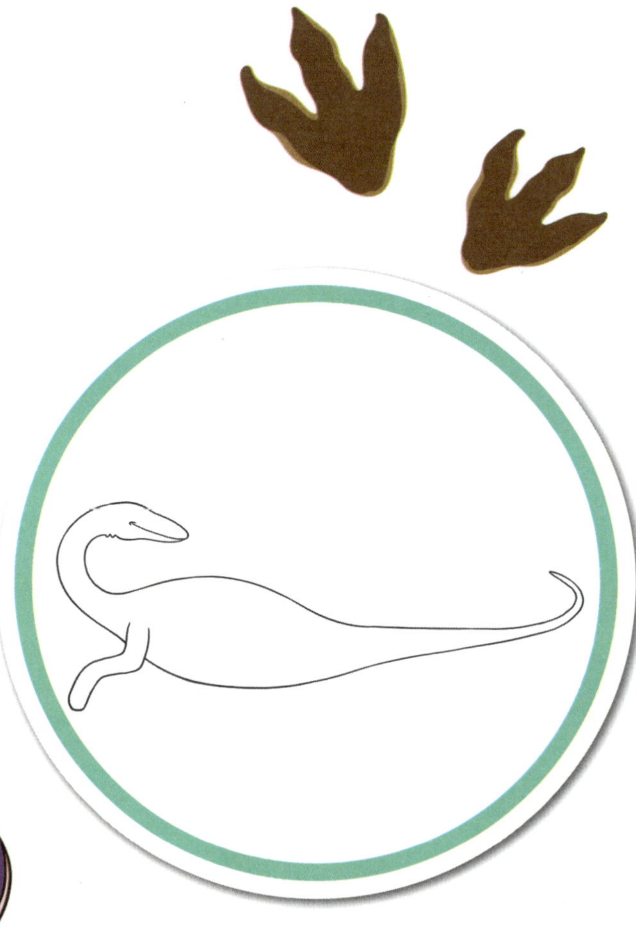

2 Draw the arm. Draw the lower body and extend it to make a tail.

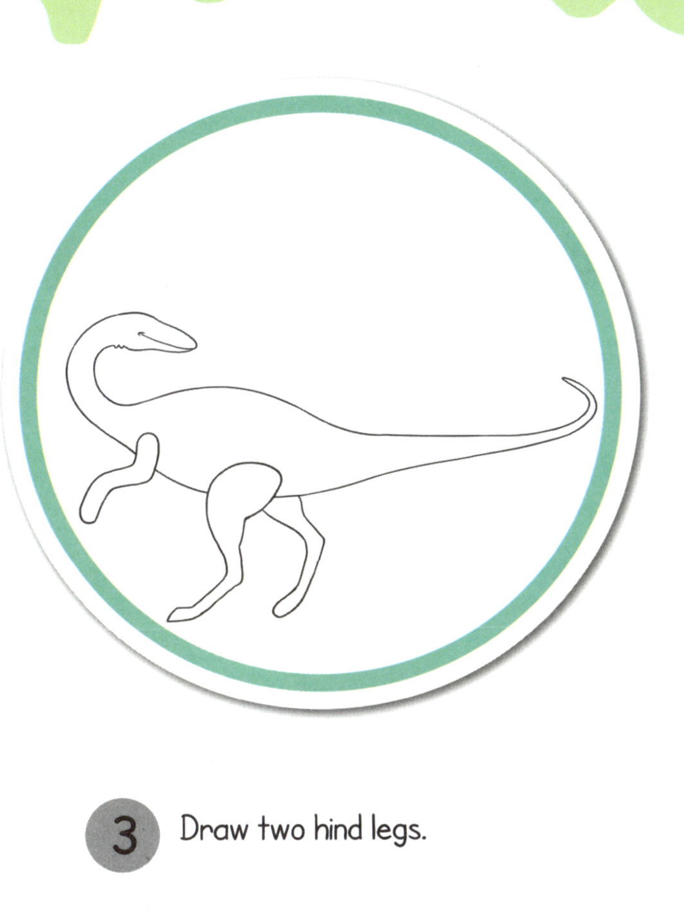

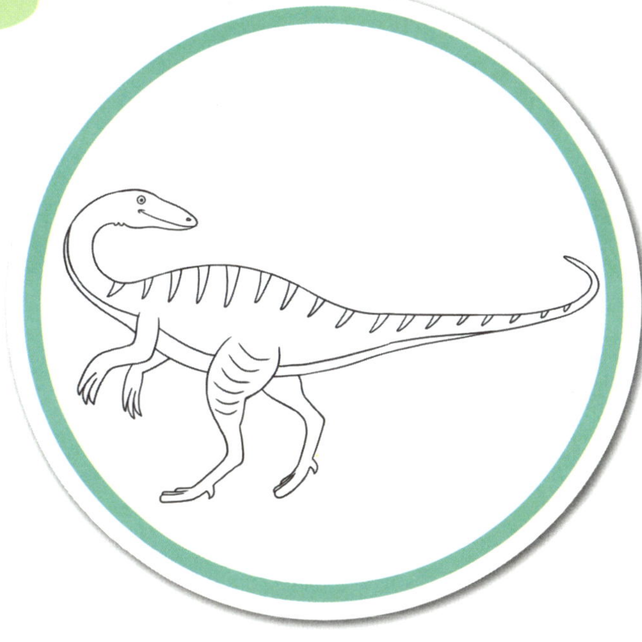

4 Draw the eye and nostril. Draw the remaining arm, fingers and feet. Draw stripes. Colour to complete.

3 Draw two hind legs.

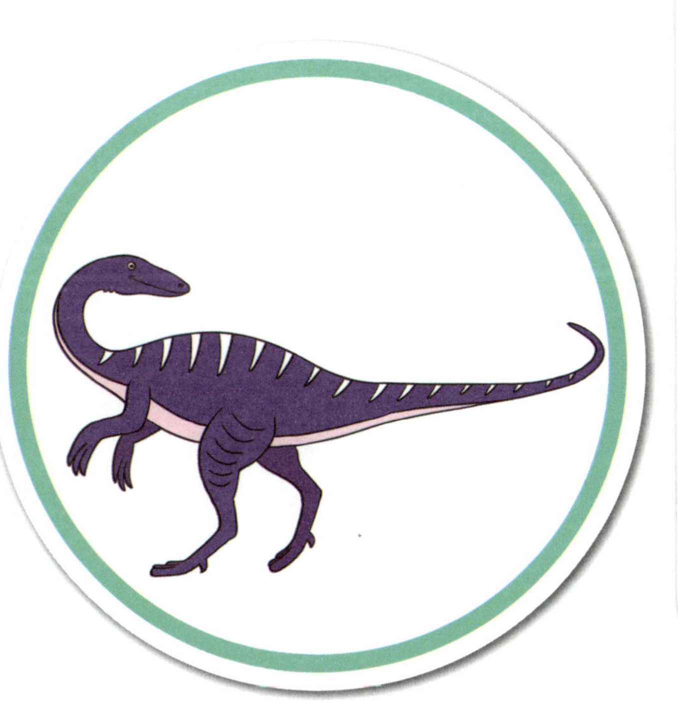

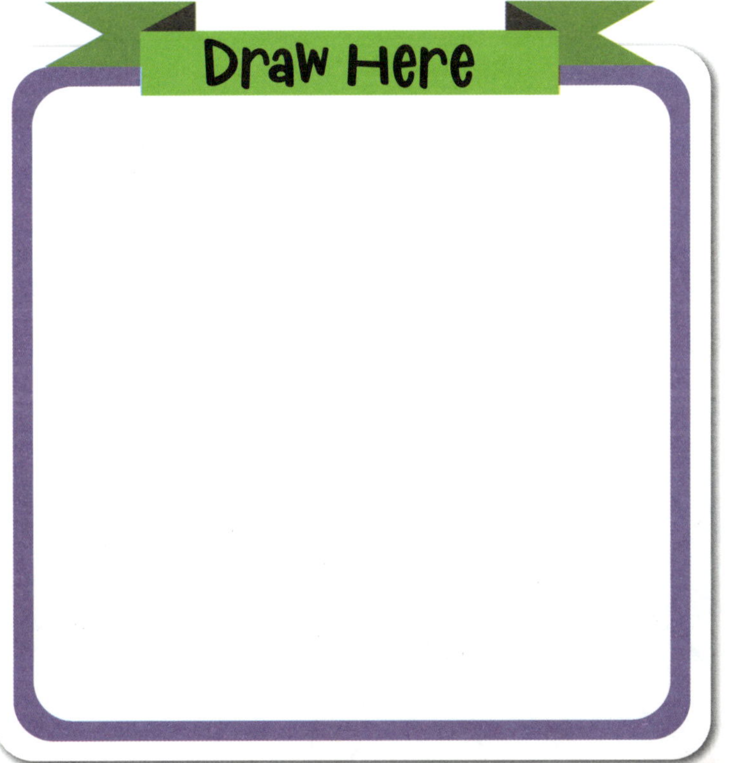

ICHTHYOSAURUS

This is an Ichthyosaurus.
It was a marine reptile and
a cousin to the dinosaurs.

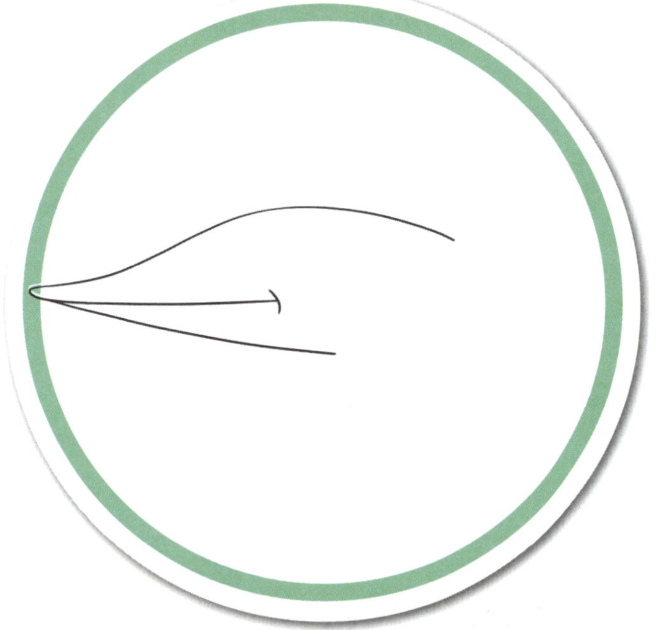

1 Draw the shape of a fish face and a mouth.

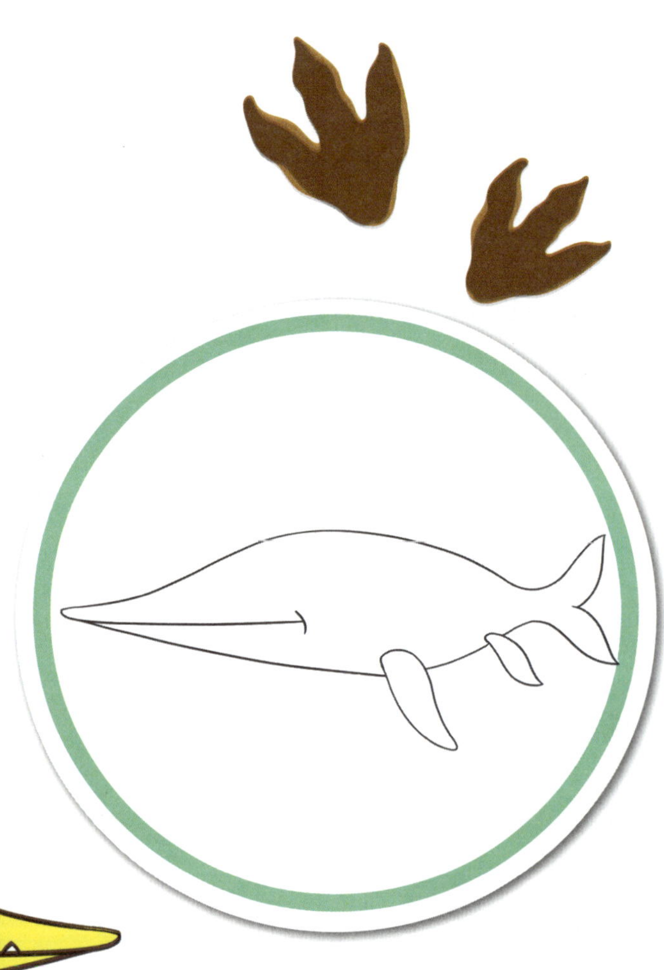

2 Extend the lines to make the body. Draw a tail and fins.

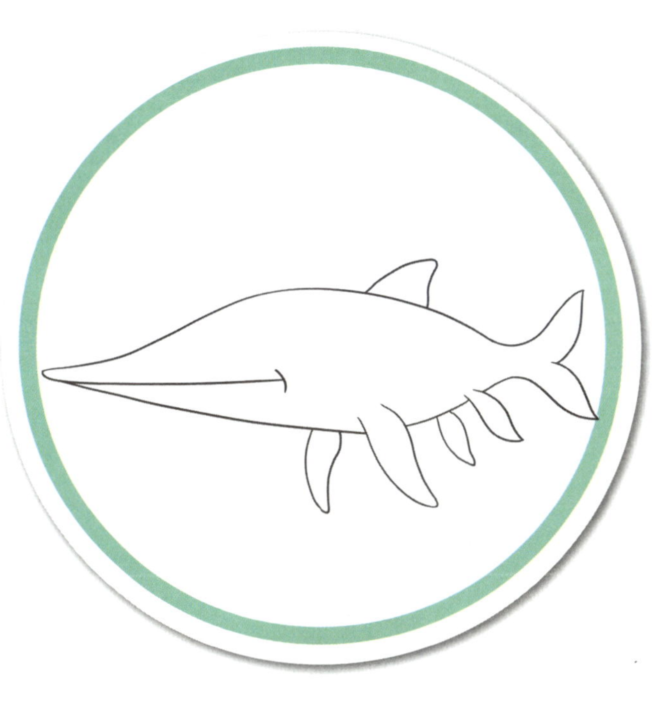

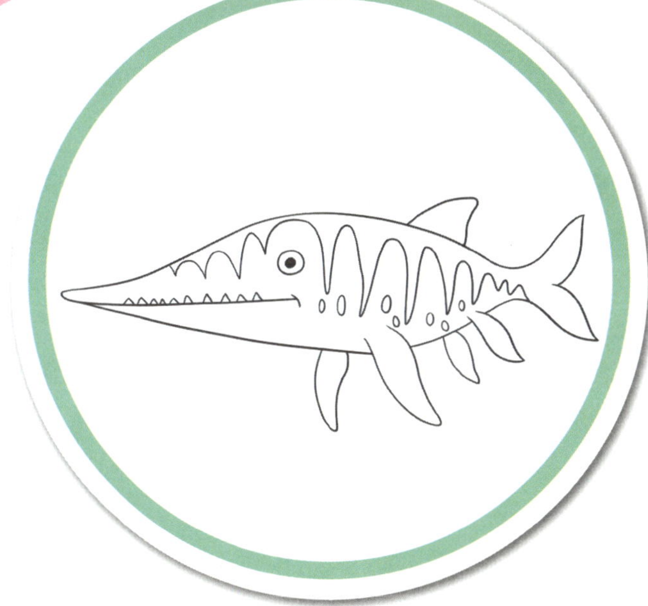

4 Draw the eye, teeth, zigzag design and circles on the fish. Colour to complete.

3 Draw the remaining fins.

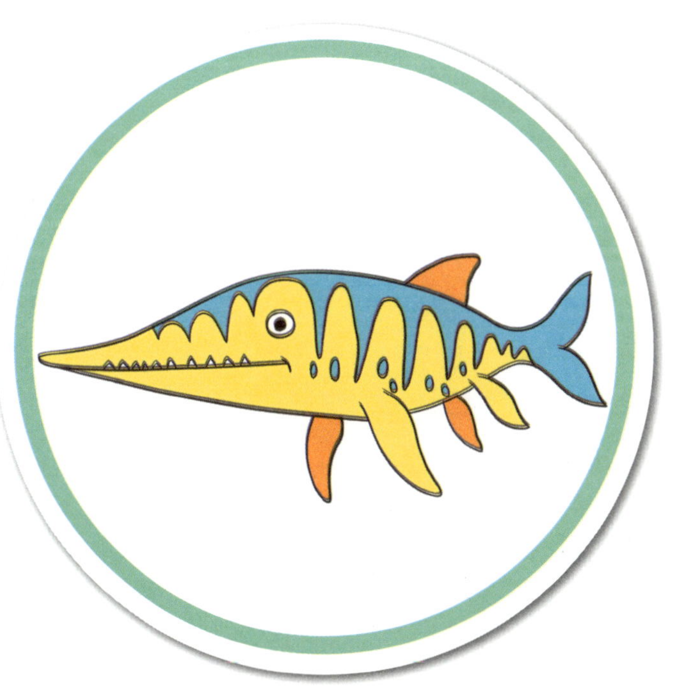

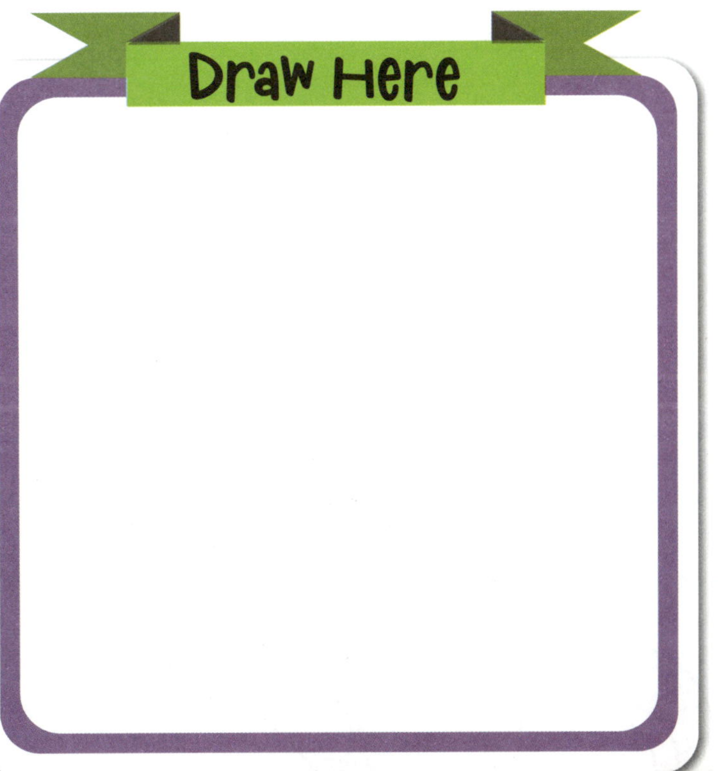

CARNOTAURUS

This is Carnotaurus. It was a meat-eating dinosaur with two horns.

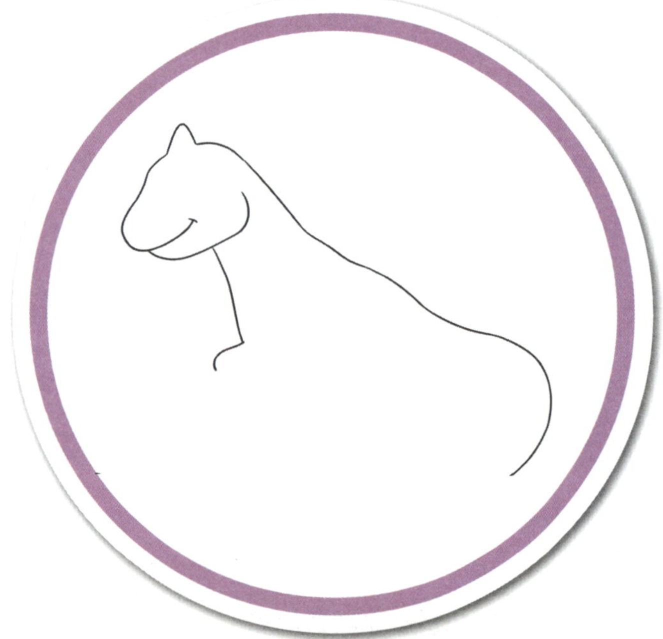

1 Draw a face with a horn and mouth. Extend the line from the face to form the body.

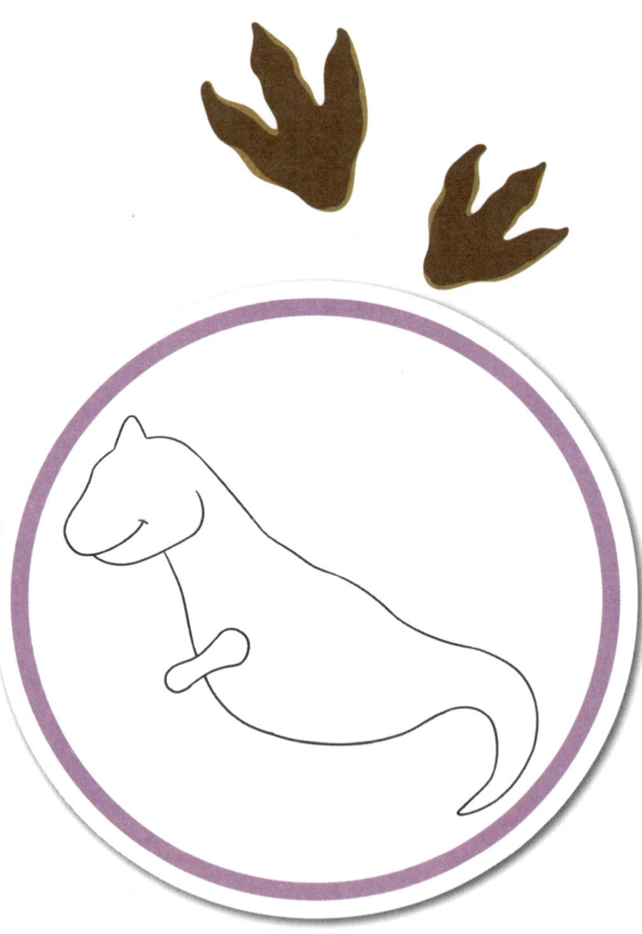

2 Draw a tail and a lower body. Draw a bone shape to make the arm.

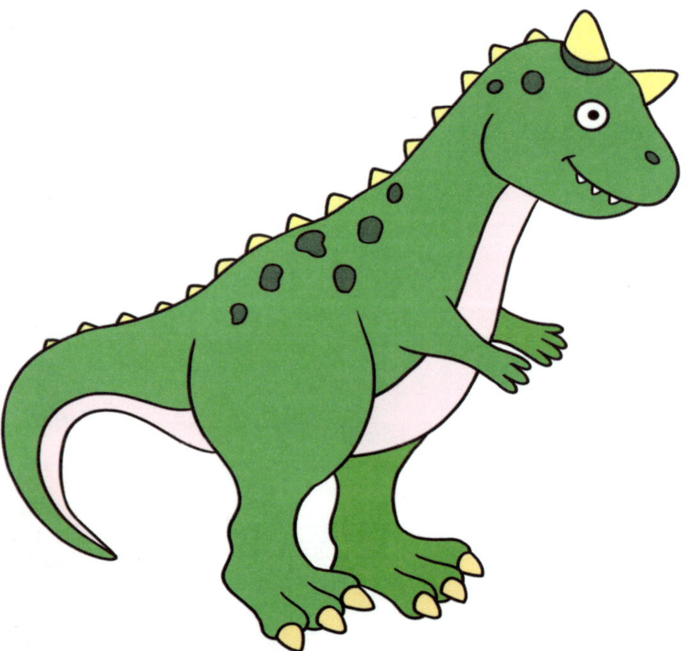

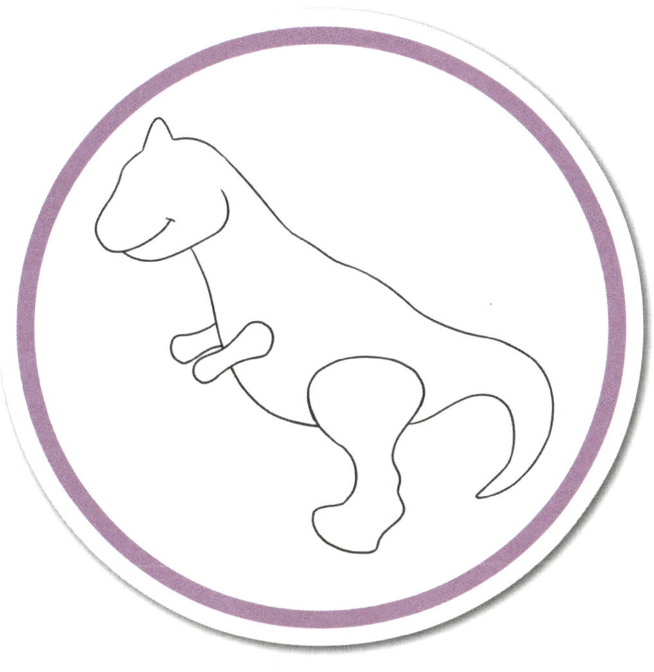

3 Draw another bone-shaped arm.
Draw the hind leg.

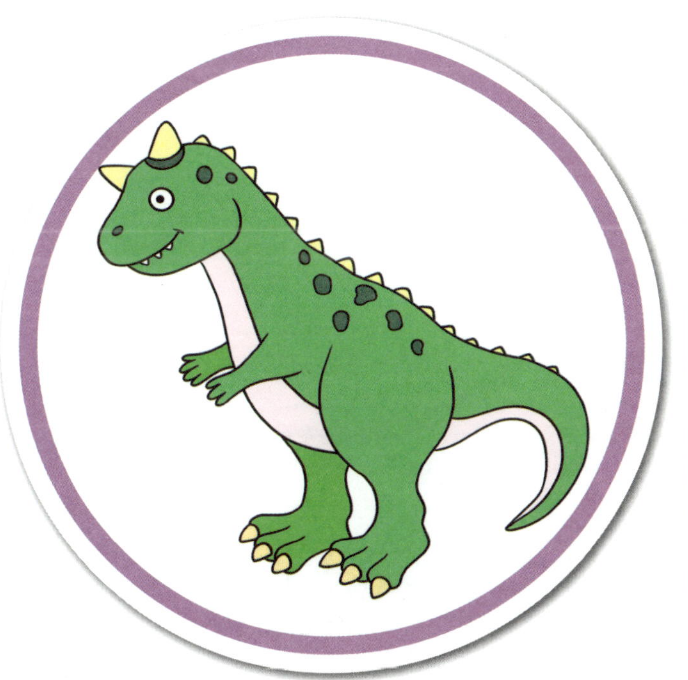

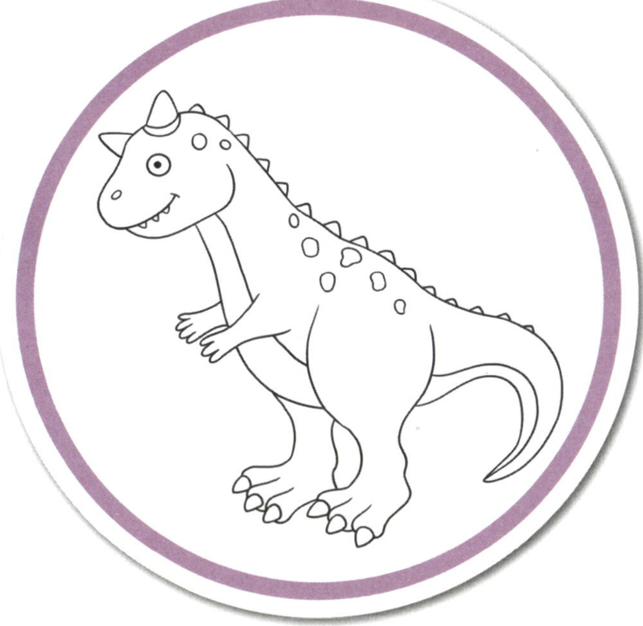

4 Draw the second horn, eye, nostril, teeth, leg, toes, fingers and spikes. Colour to complete.

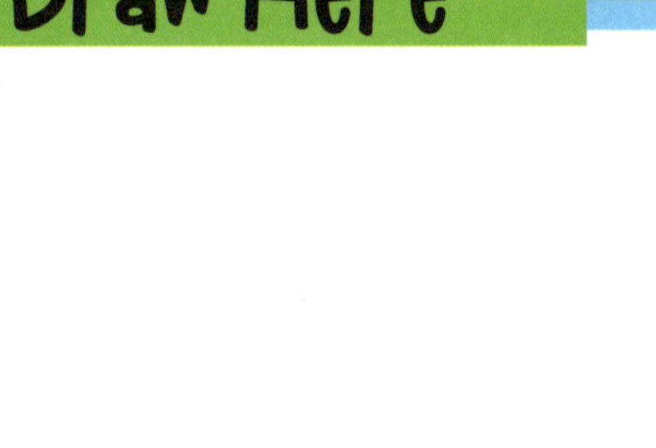

ISANOSAURUS

This is Isanosaurus. It was a herbivore in the Southeast Asian jungles.

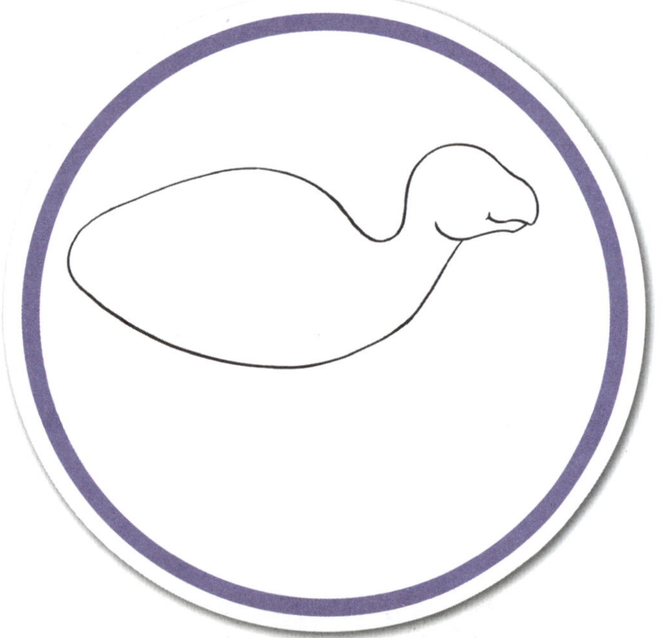

1 Draw an oval shape. On the right side, erase and extend lines to draw the head and mouth.

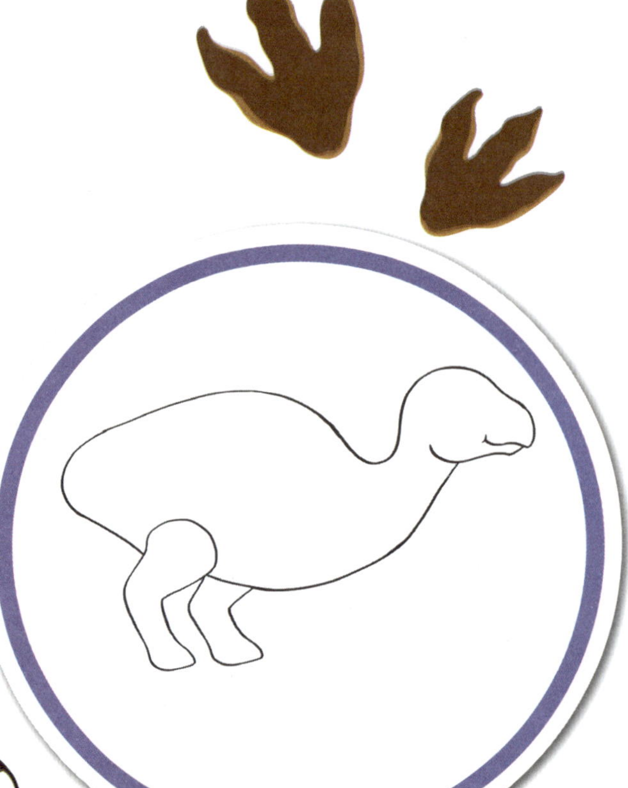

2 Draw the hind legs of the dinosaur.

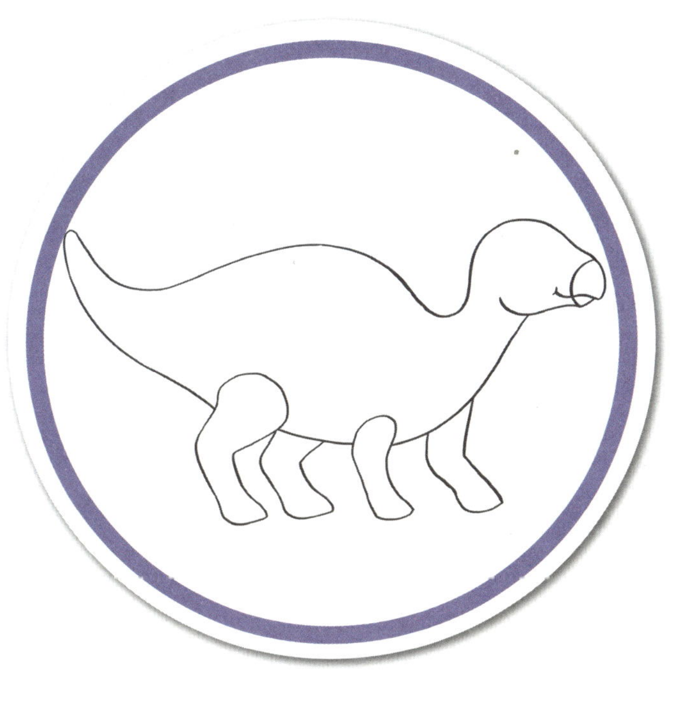

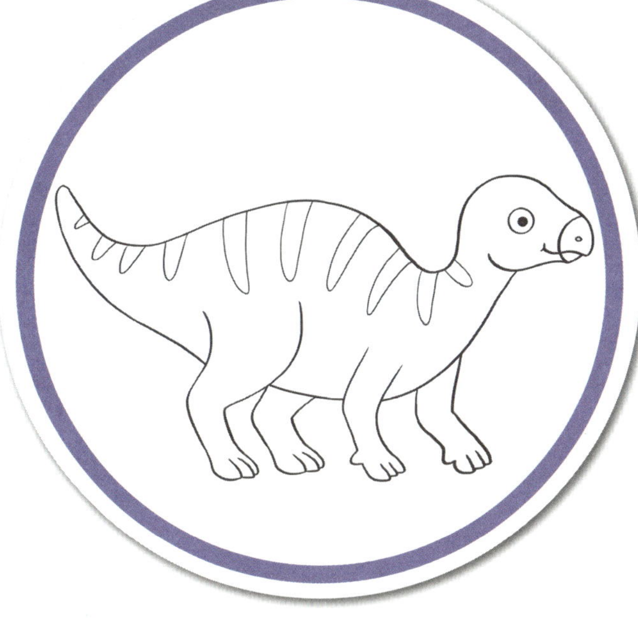

4 Draw conical stripes inside the body. Draw the eye, nostril and toes. Colour to complete.

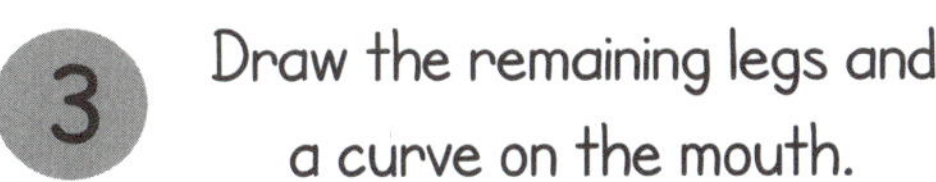

3 Draw the remaining legs and a curve on the mouth.

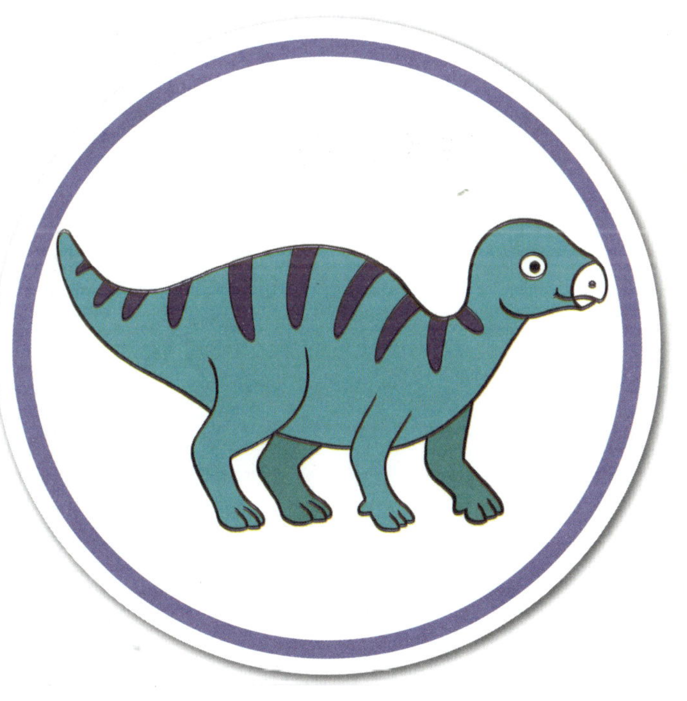

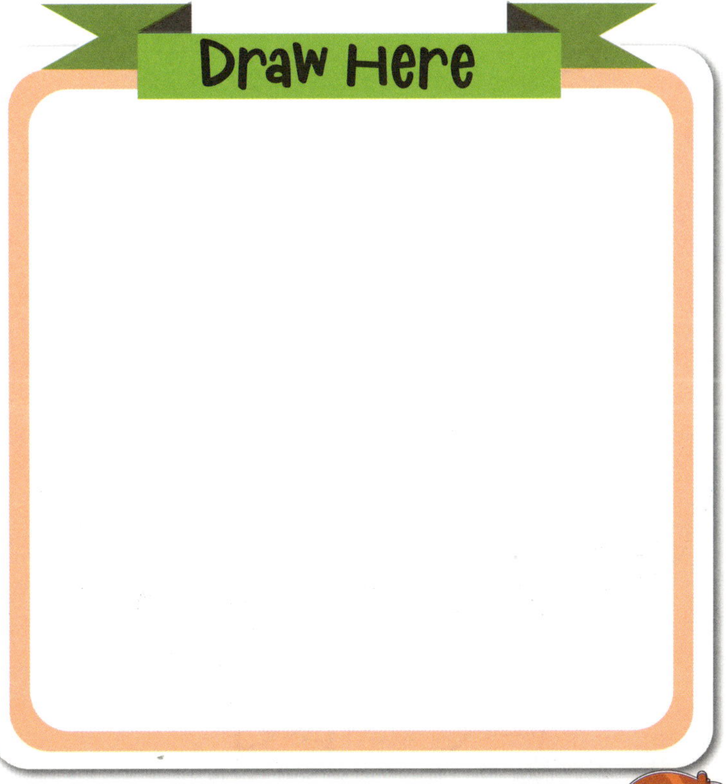

VELOCiRAPTOR

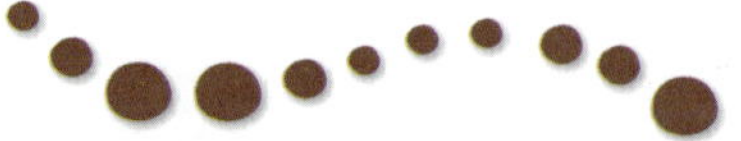

This is a velociraptor. It weighed around 100 pounds and was the size of a wolf.

1 Draw the face and upper body of the dinosaur.

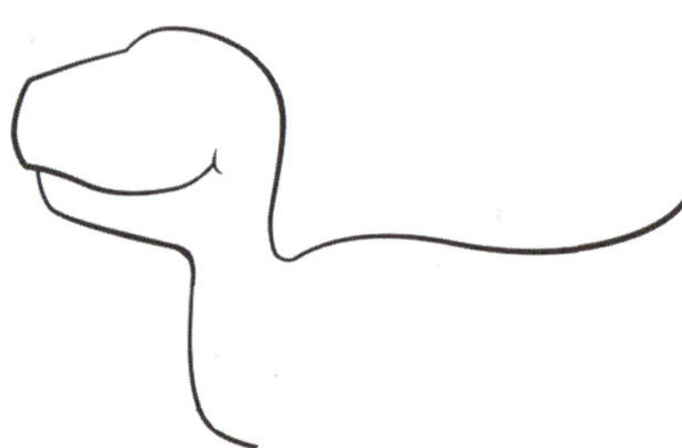

2 Draw its tail.

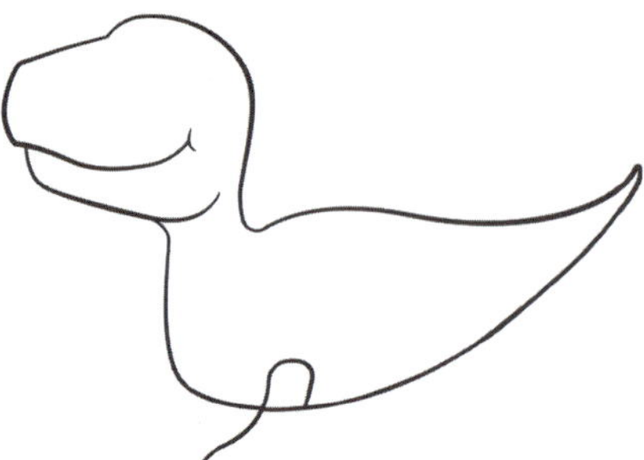

3 Draw its hands and legs.

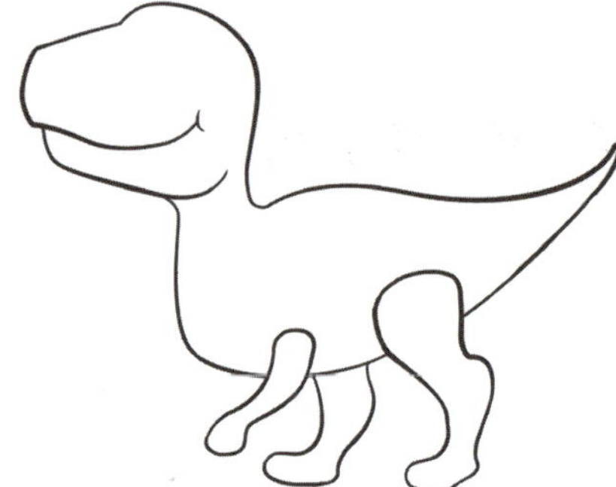

4 Draw its eyes, nose and teeth. Add details to its body and then colour to complete it.

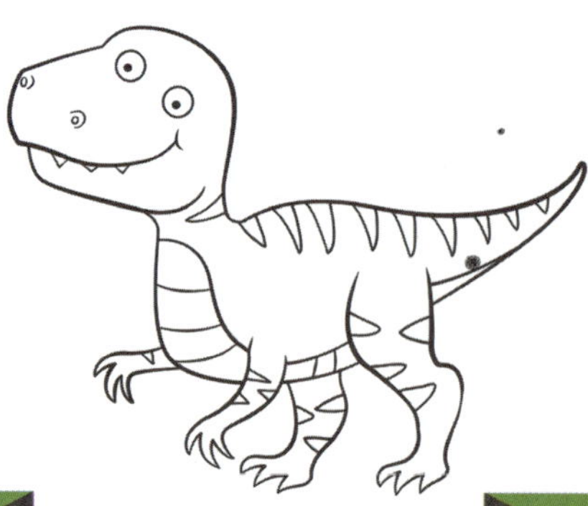

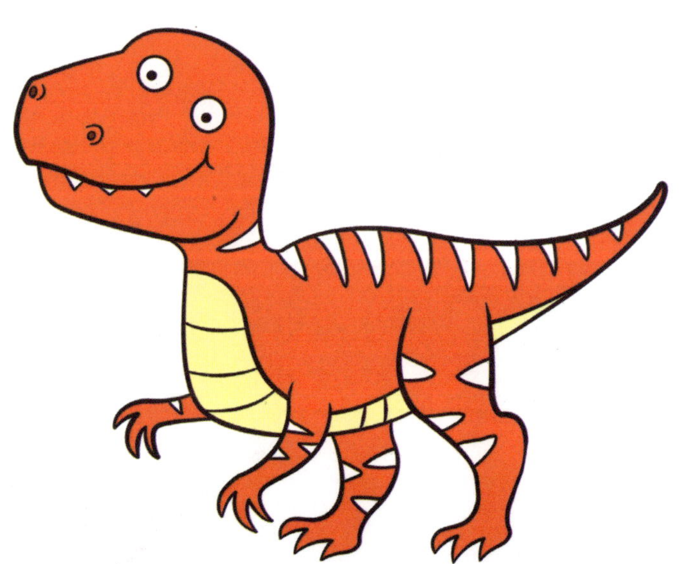

Draw Here